CHILDREN AFLOAT

AVON

CHILDREN AFLOAT

Pippa Driscoll

FERNHURST BOOKS

First published in Great Britain in 1989 by Fernhurst Books,
31 Church Road, Hove, East Sussex

ISBN 0 906754 42 9

Fernhurst Books would like to thank the following: Westerly Sea School for the loan of the Westerly Fulmar; Chris Wood of Yachtmail for the loan of equipment; Crewsaver for the loan of children's lifejackets and harnesses; Chloë and Simon Davison and Oliver and Charlotte Driscoll for allowing themselves to be photographed. The recipes in Chapter 7 are taken from *The Beaufort Scale Cookbook* by June Raper, published by Fernhurst Books.

All photographs in the text are by John Woodward, except the following: Tim Davison, page 22 (both); Pippa and John Driscoll, pages 16, 36, 44, 59, 71, 79 and 93. The cover photograph is by John Woodward.

Note that where the words 'he' or 'his' are used in the text, 'she' or 'her' are implied throughout.

Edited and designed by Joyce Chester
Typeset by Book Economy Services, Burgess Hill
Printed by Ebenezer Baylis, Worcester

Printed and bound in Great Britain

Contents

1. *Introduction*

Had I been asked five years ago whether it was a good idea for a family with two children under five to buy a 36ft yacht and go cruising, I would have said 'No'.

Now, five years on, I feel I have learnt a great deal both from the bad days and the good days. I have experienced family cruising at its best, and its worst, and I would have no hesitation in recommending cruising to other families.

If I had to start at the beginning again the experience would be even better second time around. I would insist on a bit of passage planning, plenty of pre-cruise organisation of meals, clothing and so on and a silent agreement to stick to fair weather cruising and no racing, with short passages being the order of the day.

Those of you who are terrified at the prospect of being surrounded by all that water while being responsible for small children who cannot swim, read on.

Cruising with children can be wonderfully rewarding, provided that some basic safety rules are agreed and followed, with absolutely no exceptions. Young children have no inherent fear of the sea; your confidence and your enthusiasm for the sport can be both infectious and instructive. Get it wrong, however, and you can put them off sailing for life.

Left: If everyone follows the rules a cruise with the children can be a rewarding experience for the whole family.

2. *Safety First!*

Without the peace of mind that comes from knowing your children are free from danger on board the boat, it is difficult to see how sailing can be fun. Mothers are used to concentrating on more than one thing at a time in the home, but when an element of mental panic about the safety of a child clouds the mind, this skill ceases to exist. Routine tasks such as preparing a meal, steering the boat, plotting a course or hoisting the mainsail can suddenly become unusually difficult.

On deck

LIFEJACKETS (PERSONAL FLOTATION DEVICES) AND BUOYANCY AIDS (LIFE VESTS)

A proper lifejacket (personal flotation device, PFD) will turn and support an unconscious person with their face clear of the water, whereas a buoyancy aid (life vest) simply aids someone in the water. Clearly a lifejacket is safer, but what if you cannot get your child to wear a full BSI lifejacket (US Coast Guard approved PFD) because it's too bulky, looks dreadful and isn't the right size? Add to that the fact that some manufacturers don't submit their lifejackets for British Standards Institute testing because of the expense and you, the buyer, are left with a big problem.

Working on the principle that the least effective lifejacket is the one that is left in a locker, we overcame the problem when our children were both under five by choosing buoyancy aids (life vests) which provided the best compromise. Buoyancy aids (life vests) for young children tend to be made with collars which give the support needed

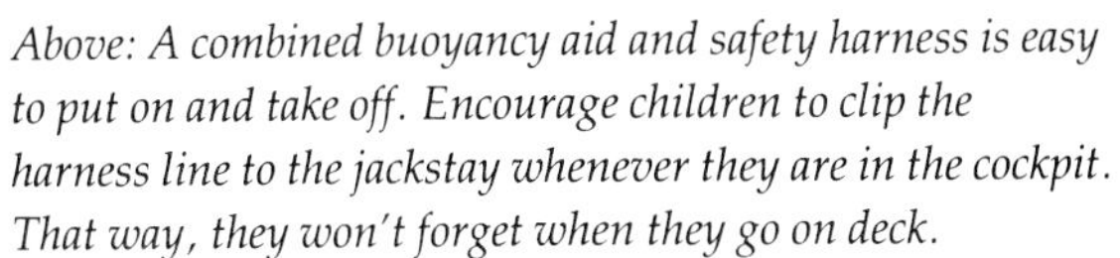

Above: A combined buoyancy aid and safety harness is easy to put on and take off. Encourage children to clip the harness line to the jackstay whenever they are in the cockpit. That way, they won't forget when they go on deck.

Right: Children must learn to inflate their lifejackets unaided. This type has enough solid foam buoyancy to support the child in the water, but it is much more efficient when topped up with air.

to keep their heads out of the water, but they are not so bulky that they restrict movement.

When buying a lifejacket look for one with the BSI kitemark on it (in the UK) or one which is US Coast Guard approved (in US) and use one that is the right size for your child. You must accept that, just as with all children's clothing, garments that are too small will have to be discarded for larger sizes as your child grows up. It could be fatal to attempt the false economy of buying too large a lifejacket. Not only will it feel uncomfortable and restrict your child's movement, but if it cannot be secured properly, it will not support him effectively in the water.

SAFETY HARNESSES

Non-swimmers need confidence about the boat, and it is essential that no unnecessary risks are taken while sailing. Properly used, a safety harness can give confidence to both child and parent and will not restrict his freedom.

Until children reach the size where they can wear one of the proprietary junior safety harnesses you will have to improvise. We modified a standard toddler's walking harness by removing the reins and firmly attaching a suitable length of line. It is obviously important that a young toddler cannot undo the quick release hook for himself!

By the time the children are about three, you can move on to one of the standard junior harnesses, but you may need to shorten the line. If your boat is fitted with an adequate harness jackstay on each side of the deck, young children really only need a line long enough to let them reach the cockpit from the deck without your having to unclip them. An older child needs a longer harness line, allowing him plenty of freedom about the boat but short enough to keep his head clear of the water should he fall oveboard.

Harnesses should also be worn on deck while in the marina or at anchor. Lifejackets are essential when transferring from or to the boat and at the water's edge on a pontoon or quay. It is definitely not worth taking any risks. An older child who is a confident swimmer, however, would probably be insulted to have to wear a lifejacket

Above: For younger children, replace the hook at the harness end with a simple loop: push this through the anchor point and thread the line back through.

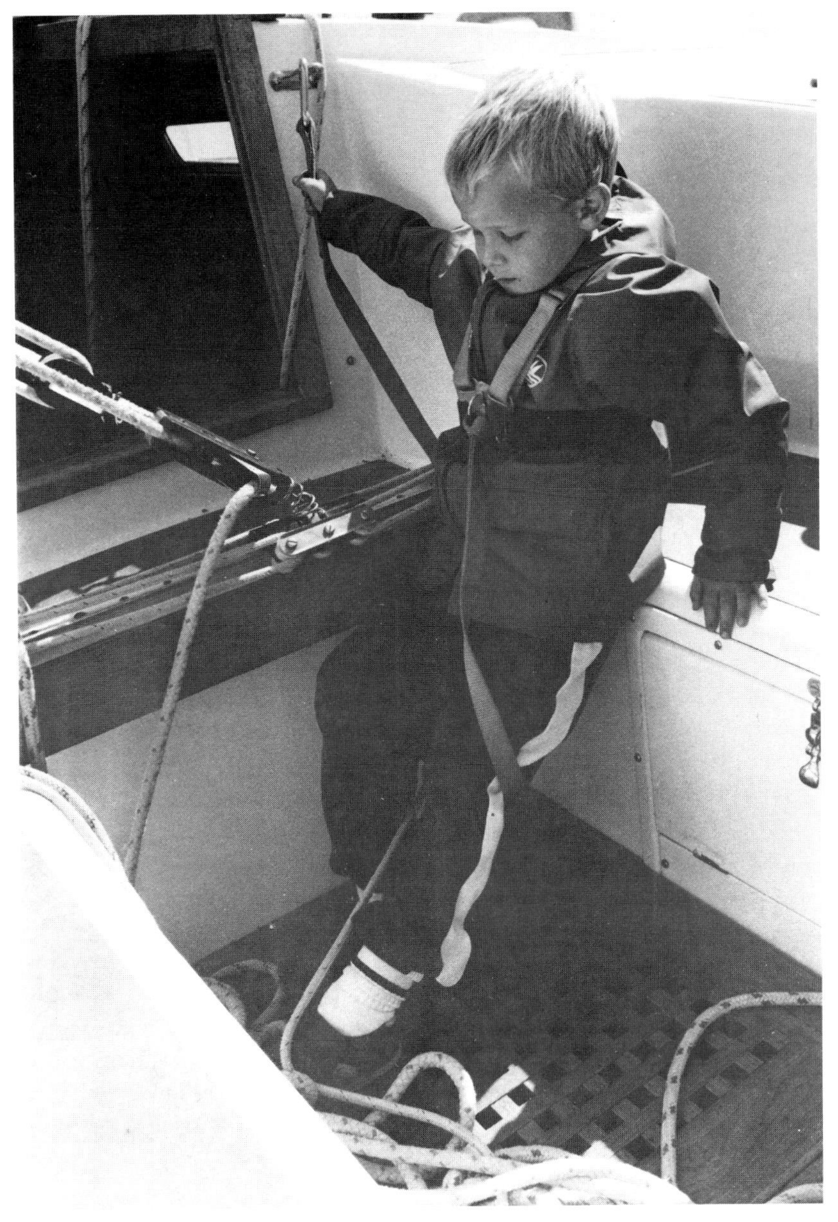

Right: A harness anchorage point beside the main hatch provides security for children coming on deck. Make sure they hook on before leaving the cabin.

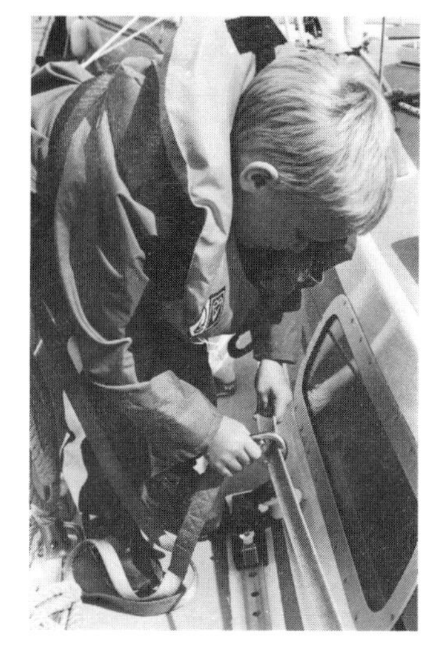

Above: children should always be securely clipped on to the jackstay if they venture outside the cockpit.

Right: If you secure the harness line to the anchor point on the windward side it will stop the child falling far if he slips.

while fishing from the pontoon in a shallow marina. Ultimately the decision is yours.

NETTING

Safety on deck, as far as we are concerned, is one of the most important things to consider. Provided your child has his harness on, he can come to very little harm apart from the occasional bump or bruise and getting tangled in the rigging and around the winches. To provide extra security from the risk of falling overboard it is possible

Left: Netting stretched between the guardrail and the toerail keeps children, toys and even sails safely aboard.

to buy netting from the chandler, which is attached from the toe-rails to the guardrails. The netting also stops toys and other treasures slipping overboard, unless they are deliberately thrown. The only disadvantage is aesthetic: for netting can really destroy the elegant lines of a yacht. But surely it is worth losing that elegance temporarily for the sake of your family's security.

Below deck

LEECLOTHS

Children love the idea of their own special bunk where they can have all their favourite things around them. It is worth making the bunk inviting, safe and comfortable. When under way a leecloth or leeboard prevents the child and his treasured possessions from falling

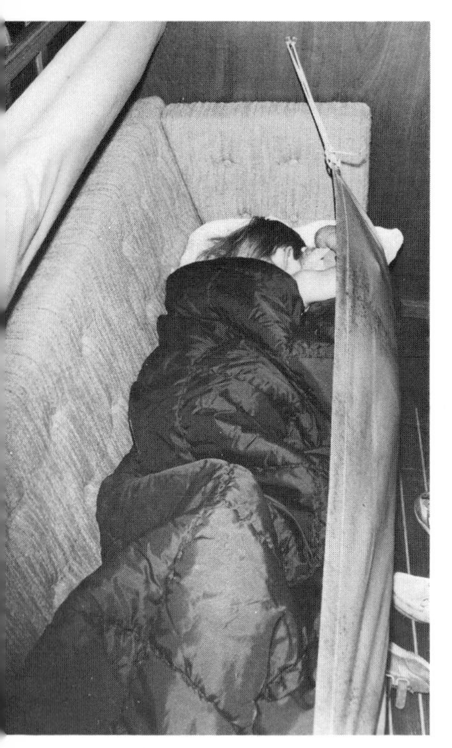

Above: Leecloths or leeboards are essential for sleeping underway. They can also be used to provide a secure play area when you need to know that the children are safe.

out. (For the various alternatives to conventional leecloths, see Chapter 5.) The bunk is also a useful place for a child when the boat is undergoing difficult manœuvres, or in a sudden downpour of rain or if the child simply needs a rest.

COMPANIONWAY

Given the choice, the companionway steps should be gently sloping and easy for children to negotiate, both going up and down. We were put off buying one boat purely because the companionway steps were too steep and the thought of having to carry the children up and down each time was too much for me. We got the children themselves to test the steps for us and on our Westerly Conway they were easily managed by an active two-year-old.

COOKER

In the cabin, where space is so important, the cooker is usually accessible from a number of directions. Remember that it is accessible to a child as well: for example, the top burners of many cookers can be reached from the main saloon bunk. The only sensible solution is to have a rule that children must *never* touch the cooker or anything on it. (In passing, we also have a rule that the cook must always wear oilskins when cooking at sea.)

Above: Children – and adults too – often come to grief when trying to climb down the companionway steps in a seaway. If they try to climb down facing forward like this they are particularly insecure.

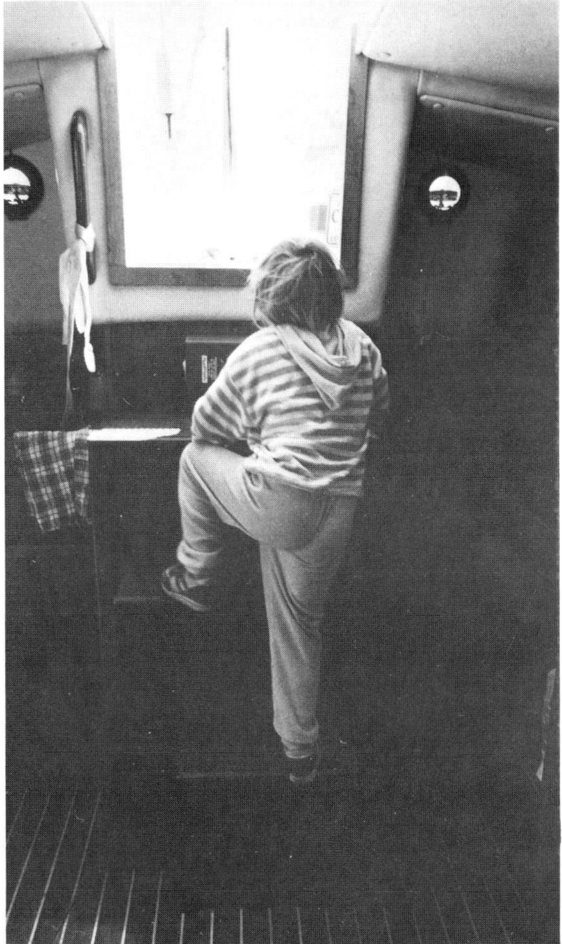

Above: Teach your children to face the steps or ladder when going up or down the companionway, since this allows them to hang on tight. It's a good idea to check that the children can negotiate the steps when you're choosing a boat.

Rules under way

Every family will have to make its own rules according to the size of the boat, the cruising area and the ages of their children. For our own peace of mind and enjoyment we keep the rules simple but rigid.

Harnesses and buoyancy aids (life vests) are worn on deck at all times by non-swimmers when the boat is under way, so that the crew can complete any manœuvre at sea or in the harbour without worrying about the children's safety. This also means that the children can see exactly what is going on at all times, rather than being banished below, and can help with most manœuvres according to their age and ability.

However, there are times when children are happier down below. An open sea passage can become boring after a while, especially if it

Right: Well padded with sleeping bags and protected from the wind and rain, the coachroof under the spray hood can become a snug haven for children who don't like to be banished below.

is cold or raining. Given the alternative of playing below in a warm, dry, secure bunk, most children (and their mothers!) need little persuasion.

One compromise, which our children enjoy, is to snuggle on the coachroof (trunk) under the spray hood. With the main hatch cover closed, this becomes their 'house' for play, some meals, and even naps when padded out with sleeping bags and pillows. This has the added advantage for me that they stay in oilies and harnesses, so that I don't have the repeated chore of dressing and undressing them. Against that, we have to keep them supplied with food, toys and books.

Safety at anchor – swimming and rowing

In the right conditions, an anchored yacht provides an excellent base for swimming: away from the crowds on the beach, you can have the water to yourselves. Older children may want to swim at virtually every anchorage but you must lay down some sensible rules.

Never allow swimming when there is anything more than a trickle of tide running through the anchorage. The average swimmer can manage a couple of knots for a short time but will soon get tired. If you are in doubt about the strength of tide when anchored, check the log.

Make sure you rig the boarding ladder or a rope ladder before going swimming. It is impossible for someone in the water to pull himself aboard the smallest of cruising yachts because of the height of freeboard – the amount of hull out of the water.

You might also consider streaming a line astern so that tired swimmers can simply grab it to pull themselves back to the boat. If you don't carry a floating line, make a warp float with a spare fender or two.

If a quiet anchorage provides older children with the joys of swimming, it also gives younger ones the perfect place to start learning how to row. The simple pleasure of rowing an inflatable

AVON
AVON

dinghy keeps some children amused for hours. Insist on buoyancy aids (life vests) for all non- and weak swimmers and consider tethering the dinghy to the yacht with a very long, light line. (This is not to be recommended in a crowded anchorage unless you want the task of unravelling a cat's cradle of line from around all the other boats.)

Several friends of ours have resorted to carrying two or even three small dinghies for days like these – but reserve the one with an outboard engine as a rescue boat!

Far left: A quiet anchorage or mooring can provide an ideal opportunity for the children to practise their rowing. But make sure they wear buoyancy aids, and attach a long line to the dinghy for safety.

Transferring to and from the dinghy

Potentially the most hazardous part of cruising with small children is transferring to and from the dinghy. It should, however, become just another routine if you stay calm and don't try to rush things.

There are a few things you can do to make life a little bit easier for yourselves. The most important point is to *secure the dinghy alongside.* Never, ever, try to hold a dinghy alongside and transfer a child from or to it.

Secondly, ensure that one adult goes first, whether it is down into the dinghy or up into the yacht.

The next point is to work out a loading plan for the dinghy and then insist that children sit down where you have told them and remain still, with fingers inside the dinghy's gunwale.

A strong boarding ladder firmly secured makes life much easier, whatever the age of the children. We abandoned a cheap, plastic folding one in favour of a strong, stainless steel model once the children started to climb it on their own.

A break in the guardrails on each side of the boat, with quick-release hooks on the 'gate' saves you having to climb over, possibly carrying the children and gear.

To get a baby ashore, using a typical inflatable yacht tender, it is safer for two people to be involved. One person attends to the baby and the other to the boat. Toddlers are best carried down the ladder

Above: Never let children attempt to climb back on board unaided. When they come back from a rowing expedition make sure one adult is on hand to get down into the dinghy to help them up the side of the yacht.

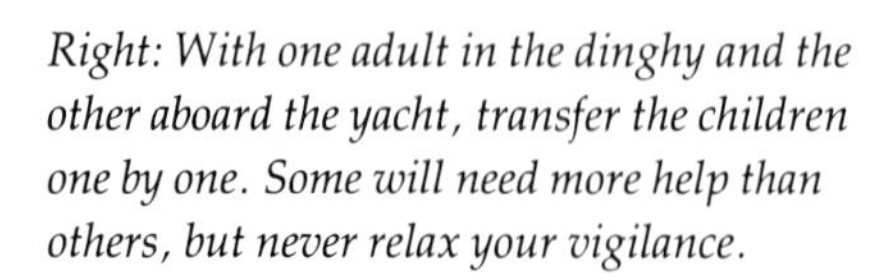

Right: With one adult in the dinghy and the other aboard the yacht, transfer the children one by one. Some will need more help than others, but never relax your vigilance.

Left: A permanent stern boarding ladder is a good investment, and may save a life if someone falls overboard. Make sure it is a strong design; some of the temporary folding types will collapse under the weight of a grown man.

or passed from one adult to another. Older children enjoy the challenge and excitement of the transfer and should be encouraged to take care of themselves.

Once your children reach the age when they can row the dinghy, putting them in charge of the whole operation provides them with a valuable lesson in being the skipper.

One of the worst prospects facing the cruising parent with small children is having to scale a high harbour wall at low water by means of a slimy ladder. Tiny babies travel by sling; older children manage for themselves. It is the toddler and young child that prove the greatest difficulty.

A backpack may be suitable for small toddlers, but once a child can

Left: Always encourage the child to look after himself, but stand by to give support – moral as well as physical – if needed.

scale a ladder, the parent best acts as a safety net, positioned around the child.

Finally, consider the possibility of using the bosun's chair for getting children up and down when lying alongside a harbour wall. Once again, you need an adult at both ends and a line attached to the bosun's chair to pull it across from mast to quay. This was exactly the way we saw a youngster with an injured foot being taken ashore in one West Country harbour.

In a similar way a bucket on a halyard can be used for transferring equipment up and down a wall.

Left: Using a slippery, weed-covered ladder to get up a high harbour wall can be an alarming prospect. Climb up just behind each child to shield him or her from the danger of falling.

cassette tapes. The motion of the boat often helps them to doze off, even during the day, though the extra exertion of shore visits, lots of fresh air and early starts to catch the tide may also make them more sleepy than usual. Older children will help out with the sailing and enjoy more sophisticated games, while the excitement and challenge of fishing for their lunch will keep many involved for hours.

There is no doubt that a happy atmosphere and contented crew makes for enjoyable cruising. Don't forget that life on board presents parent–child relationships in a totally new light to the conventional ones ashore. A child who has never seen his parents under stress at work, for example, will see them having to face direct responsibility and make immediate decisions, sometimes when cold, wet, tired and frightened.

Similarly, children could find that their parents have more time to devote to their needs and to play with them, being away from the distractions of modern day living ashore. Often, too, the conventional parental roles are reversed, with deckwork and domestic duties being shared equally.

Finally, don't forget that there could be a fundamental difference in mental attitude towards the boat herself between your children and yourselves. What you see as a hard-earned pleasure and a place to relax may be viewed with long-suffering patience by a child who would rather be somewhere else. Living in a confined space is especially difficult for many younger children, whose natural inclination is towards the freedom of wide open spaces – not an unending vista of grey sea.

Your attitude in planning your sailing, possibly making compromises in order to accommodate the needs of your family, will be reflected in their greater love, enjoyment and enthusiasm for the sport.

4. *Clothing*

It is easy to spend a small fortune on clothing a sailing family, particularly if you aim to follow the trends set by the specialist clothing manufacturers. Our experience is that we can equip the children perfectly adequately for a fraction of the cost by using a mixture of new yachting clothing, children's clothing from ordinary shops and borrowed or second-hand gear.

Waterproofs

Cruising demands that you and your family spend a lot of time outside, often in exposed conditions. During a downpour or even in persistent mist your children, without waterproofs of some description, will get very wet and cold. Babies and toddlers are unlikely to need 'real' waterproofs and an all-in-one suit of the kind you can purchase from most children's clothes shops is more than adequate. Your child probably has one already in his extensive wardrobe.

As they get older and a lot more active, it is probably worth buying a proper set of waterproofs from the chandler. Douglas Gill have a good range of jackets and trousers to fit children of 18 months upwards. They come in different colours and there are even sailing wellies to match, though ordinary ones are adequate.

Clothing in general

On board, underneath their waterproofs, their clothing should be warm, comfortable, easy to get on and off and easy to wash. Track

Far left: Keeping the children warm, dry and comfortable is half the battle. Kit them out with waterproofs and tracksuits, and flat shoes with non-slip soles.

suits get my vote, with a shirt underneath and large sweaters to go over the top to give an extra layer. Children are much happier with their arms and legs unrestricted and they need to be able to move about easily and feel relaxed. Experts in most outdoor activities recognise the principle of keeping warm by wearing several layers of clothing.

For fine weather wear your children probably already possess suitable shoes. Make sure they wear a pair with flat, non-slip soles that give a good grip when they clamber about on deck.

It is important to remember a sun-hat for your children. It can be deceptively cool in the summer in a marina with a sea breeze blowing and when sailing, but these are the very times when children are most likely to get burnt. Little heads and shoulders burn very easily so, in addition to the sun-hats, keep a good children's sun block on board.

How much?

Of course what you take and how much you take depends on the particular needs of your family. Clothing children over three means taking a set of clothes for each day away, with a couple of spare changes. The twos and under are a little more difficult as nappies (diapers) and sickness are more common, requiring more changes.

There has been a great improvement in the absorbency of disposable nappies over the last few years which is an advantage when cruising. Not only is it more comfortable for the baby but it also saves the clothes getting wet. Take plenty of plastic bags to wrap soiled nappies in before disposal.

5. *Setting up the Boat*

It is perfectly possible to modify any yacht to make family sailing more enjoyable. But you can make life even easier for yourself by choosing the right boat in the first place.

Choosing a boat

Below: A twin-keel, or even twin-hull boat that stays upright when the tide goes out is a huge advantage when cruising with children in tidal waters.

Our criterion when choosing a new cruising boat was simple – and we found that it limited our choice drastically. We decided that we

wanted two keels – for ease of drying out on beaches and to avoid any worries about unintentional drying out.

We also decided that we needed three cabins – so that the children's sleeping accommodation and our own are both separate from the main saloon. This means that our sleeping and waking times do not have to be synchronised with those of the children. Not only does this give us a great deal of freedom when cruising *en famille* but it also gives us the flexibility to take another family of four away for cruises and still get all the children to bed at a reasonable hour.

To accomplish that simple specification within our limited budget meant that we had to buy secondhand. That's no problem as long as you do your homework beforehand and narrow down the choice to prevent wasted trips to see unsuitable boats. A report from a reputable marine surveyor removes the risks of buying secondhand. A used boat is often sold with a great deal of the extra gear needed before a standard boat can really be said to be ready for sea. This can be a significant advantage when money is tight.

If you are able to buy a new boat, there are two rules to follow. The first is to spend only eighty per cent of your available budget on the boat itself; the rest of your money will be needed for extra items of essential equipment.

The second is to be prepared to detail your requirements to the boatbuilder, so that any necessary modifications can be incorporated into the specification at an early stage. Some examples of what I mean are outlined below.

On deck

HARNESSES

The importance of safety harnesses and jackstays has already been mentioned in Chapter 2. It is worth emphasising their value here, as you won't be able to relax and enjoy your cruising if you are uneasy about non-swimmers falling overboard.

Harness jackstays are simply taut lines of wire, rope or webbing

Left: Clipping the harness line to a jackstay running the length of the side deck allows an adult or responsible child to move freely about the boat, confident that there is no danger of falling overboard. But you have to follow the track of the jackstay (above) or the harness line will snag on the shrouds.

running along each side deck from bow to stern. On a small yacht it is often possible to clip your safety harness line to the jackstay before leaving the safety of the main companionway. Once clipped on, you can move freely about the deck without having to worry about the harness.

On larger yachts (or for smaller children) a harness anchorage point in the cockpit adjacent to the companionway is needed for easy access. The jackstays should be shackled to strongpoints bolted to the deck at bow and stern. We found polyester webbing perfect for jackstays because it doesn't roll underfoot.

While on the subject of deck gear, one modification worth incorporating from the start is a 'gate' in the guardrails on each side somewhere near the cockpit and another at the stern, all secured by lines with quick-release pelican hooks. Although most children

Above: As the child comes up the companionway she should have her harness on and the harness line ready to clip to the anchorage point.

Above: Make sure she clips on before she leaves the relative safety of the companionway. It is well worth fitting an anchorage point next to the hatch.

Above: Once clipped on she can step out confidently, and devote all her attention to negotiating hazards such as the main traveller.

Above: Lifting a child on and off a yacht can be an awkward, back-breaking and occasionally hazardous business.

Above: A break in the guardrails saves your back and gives the children more independence in the marina.

3.5

quickly learn to swing under or through normal guardrails, the gate makes life much easier when you are boarding or leaving a dinghy or when you are lifting children aboard or ashore.

THE DINGHY

As for the dinghy, it's worth pampering yourself with a few little luxuries. A small light outboard engine doesn't take up much space aboard and uses very little fuel, but will really make its presence felt if you ever anchor or moor far from a beach or jetty. You could also argue that it is a positive safety feature; if you are using an outboard instead of rowing you are less likely to risk overloading the dinghy to avoid a second round trip and you'll be less tired.

As well as an outboard, invest in a set of floorboards for the dinghy. They provide extra stability and rigidity when you are under way.

The third luxury is a high-speed dinghy inflator, run from the ship's supply, which saves at least five minutes of awkward pumping

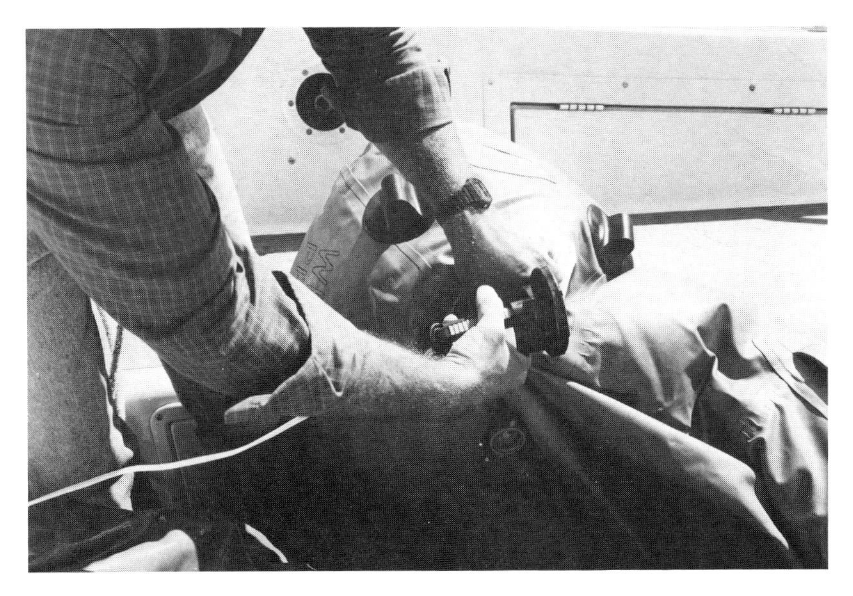

Left: A 12V high-speed dinghy inflator saves time and temper. It will also encourage you to deflate the dinghy for passage making, which in turn means faster and more trouble-free cruising. A small outboard engine (far left) is another worthwhile investment, for it takes all the sweat out of ferrying crew and stores to and fro.

every time you need the dinghy. It also sucks, enabling you to flatten the dinghy properly when the time comes to get it back into its bag to restow it in an already overcrowded locker.

BABIES AND TODDLERS

Locker space will be at a premium when you are cruising with small children, because of all the useful little extras that you will try to take along. At times, we have cruised with a pram (baby carriage) and a baby sling, and later with a buggy and a backpack.

The pram carrycot was used as a secure home for a nine-week-old baby. (The only problem was the condensation that accumulated inside it in the mornings.) We used it as a miniature bunk, wedging it firmly down a quarter berth, where the sound and warmth of a hefty diesel engine provided a soothing environment.

Although the baby sling is useful for getting little ones ashore I would not recommend its use afloat because of its effect on your balance and the danger of injury.

The buggy and the backpack are both useful if you don't want toddlers to limit your trips ashore too much; their only drawbacks are the stowage space needed and the difficulty in transferring a buggy ashore.

One other piece of child equipment regularly seen afloat is the child car seat, usually secured to the stern pulpit or fastened to a special washboard (hatchboard) slid into the companionway. While we don't find the need for one, other friends swear by them as a way of keeping small children happy and secure, where they can see everything that is going on.

DECK EQUIPMENT

So much for the special equipment; now to the way the boat herself is set up on deck. The first essential is a good spray hood, which should be standard equipment rather than an optional extra on any yacht sold in temperate climes.

Many families effectively extend their under-cover living space in harbour by means of a boom tent. This is thoroughly recommended if

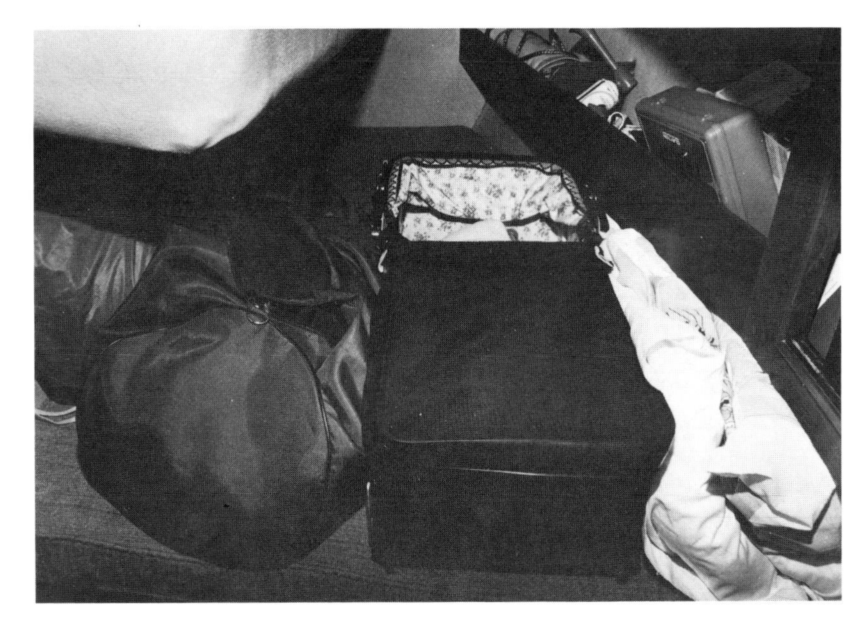

Left: The best place for a baby in a carrycot is down a quarterberth, securely wedged in with sailbags and other soft gear.

you have older children who will soon get frustrated at being cooped up below deck in bad weather. If you don't have a purpose-made tent, improvise with the storm jib secured over the boom and guyed out to the toe-rail.

Hatch covers cut out the daylight from conventional transparent cabin hatches, so that children who have to sleep while it is still light outside will not be disturbed. They are also valuable in preventing children from waking as soon as dawn breaks. Some manufacturers offer curtains on tracks as part of the hatch assembly, others offer a cover in the same material as your boom/mainsail cover which fits over the top of the hatch. Some sophisticated designs have flaps which allow you to leave the hatch ajar on warm nights.

The budget answer is to lash a spare sailbag or even a towel over the hatch. It may not look as neat, but it certainly does the job and serves as a reminder to anyone crossing your deck that there is a child asleep below.

Right: The backpack is useful for taking younger children ashore – and speeds up those shopping trips when someone wants to come along.

The rig and sail controls

Probably the most important part of setting up the boat for sailing with children is to modify the deck gear and rig according to your crew strength. While a crew that includes older children will make

light work of sail changes and anchoring, a couple sailing with young children should set the boat up so that she can be sailed single-handed. After all if one of you is unzipping a lifejacket (PFD) down below because your little darling wants to visit the heads yet again, life must still carry on above deck.

Arrange the sheet and halyard leads for ease of handling, sort out a reefing system which needs only one person on deck, and fit some sort of self-steering system, even if it is merely a piece of shock cord restraining the tiller. Make sure that essential engine instruments and the echo sounder can be seen from the steering position. Consider fitting an anchor winch and even a roller furling and reefing headsail system.

How far you go down the path of equipping the boat to your own standards will depend on your budget, but don't think of these things as luxuries. They are all intended to make life easier, so that you can enjoy the cruising more. After all, if you aren't enjoying it there's no point in being there!

Below decks

Coming down below, the first point to make is that companionways that seem easy for adults may be impossible to negotiate for some toddlers (see Chapter 2). Similarly, the height of the saloon table can be a problem for little ones. As high chairs are out of the question, try the baby's chair that clips onto the table top itself, putting the child in exactly the right position. The next stages are to use cushions, to allow the child to kneel or even resort to picnicking on the coachroof (trunk).

HEATING

Life below is far more comfortable for virtually all cruising folk, not just those with children, if you install a cabin heater. We considered a central heating system, rejected it in favour of a catalytic heater at a tenth of the cost and have been warm ever since. Quite apart from its practical use, the heater is a great boost to morale if you hit a bad spell of weather and is essential if you want to extend your cruising happily into the ends of the season.

Damp clothes and bedding dampen morale too, so take a couple of hot water bottles to warm up the sleeping bags before the children leap into them. Take plenty of large plastic bags for wrapping clothes. Even if your lockers are dry, condensation can be a nuisance.

As an extra idea for drying gloves, socks and other small items of clothing, try fitting a wire basket high in the space above your engine. (First take advice from the boatbuilder or engine manufacturer to ensure that you will not be depriving the engine of its essential airspace.)

BUNKS

And so to bed. The first battle is to keep the child in place, especially at sea. Every sea-going bunk should be fitted with a leecloth or leeboard, which unhappily are only optional extras on many boats.

When you are moored in the harbour, one option for a toddler is to use a metal bed side which slides under the mattress and works like a bookend. But this is not possible on the conventional fo'c's'le vee-berth; we solved the problem of children falling out by rigging a curtain of netting from the bunk top to the deckhead. If all else fails and you are worried about children falling out, a few sailbags strategically placed will ensure that they have a soft landing.

There are special small sleeping bags on the market now for children and they can be quite useful, particularly if two children are sharing the same bunk.

6. *Cruise Planning*

The yacht skipper planning any passage – or series of passages as part of a cruise – has a number of factors to consider. Wind direction, weather, tidal heights at departure and destination and tidal streams in between, duration of passage, ports of refuge, speed and range of yacht, stamina of crew – all of these will have a bearing on the passage plan.

When children are involved, however, the most important factor is boredom. This leads me to suggest a simple rule of thumb: 'Don't plan a passage which is longer in hours than the age of your youngest crew member in years'. In short, if the tiniest kid is seven, don't cruise for more than seven hours at one stretch.

Happily, you can ignore this rule if you have only a baby aboard, because their requirements are independent of the outside world. Indeed we found that a cruising yacht made a wonderful environment for our nine-week-old son who, with his carrycot tucked down a quarter berth, was quickly lulled to sleep by the sound of the diesel engine.

Once children start to develop their curiosity about their surroundings and begin to move around, the rule of thumb becomes a useful guide. Certainly if you have to make any long passages with young children, there really are only two fair alternatives: travel by night or send them on by another means of transport. We've tried both successfully.

Life becomes easier when the children are old enough to take a real interest in the passage making, rather than treating the cruising as the boring bit between exciting harbours or beaches. In the difficult years with small children, your skipper simply has to temper any ideas

about epic voyages with the blunt fact that bored children will create stress for their parents that will spoil everyone's enjoyment. Keep the passages short with plenty of activity en route *and* when you stop.

Sailing in areas where medium length (6–8-hour) passages are inevitable, we often find that the children use the time to play happily for a while below deck and then to doze. Their favourite spot in reasonable weather is tucked up under the spray hood, with the sliding part of the main hatch closed.

The only drawbacks to this are that it is slightly more difficult to get

Below: If the children fall asleep on passage it can make life a lot easier for their parents – but they often stay awake a lot later in the evening as a result!

below for a quick snack or a spot of navigation and that, having had the benefit of a sleep during the day, the children are wide awake in the evenings. But in some places this becomes an unlikely advantage, because it means that they are lively enough to take out for an evening meal at a civilised hour, instead of trying to get dinner at a restaurant impossibly early so that the children don't fall asleep at the table.

As a general principle, making longer passages at night takes a great deal of beating. Depending on the state of the tide and the length of the passage, the idea is that you leave either just before the children go to sleep, so that they have the excitement of the departure before settling down in their bunks, or you plan things so that they wake just before reaching your destination.

Many experienced yachtsmen prefer night passages anyway, particularly if they involve an offshore leg, because of navigational advantages. The most obvious one is that it is possible to identify a coastline more positively and at a greater distance by lighthouses and buoys than it is in daylight.

It all sounds fine in theory, but in practice you also have to take into account all the other factors of passage planning outlined above. Add to that the fact that your sailing might well be short-handed and you could find that although the children are bright, fresh and wide awake when you reach your destination, Mum and Dad are not. . . .

Be prepared

The key to successful cruise planning is detailed preparation. It is impossible to have too much advance information, provided it is accurate and up-to-date. How long you actually spend on the planning will depend on your experience and your familiarity with the area.

As an example, planning a seventy-mile passage might take an inexperienced skipper a couple of hours, whereas someone who knows the area and can quickly identify the main problems could, given the necessary tidal information, do the job in fifteen minutes.

As a cruise is made up of a number of passages, the same principle applies with just two variations. First the number of variables increases with the number of days in the cruise: suppose you want to spend an extra day in one place because the children love the beach there and the weather is fine – how will that affect the master plan?

Secondly, having worked out the first day or two of any cruise you then need to arrange the last couple of days, almost to the extent of leaving the part in the middle to look after itself. It's a rather sad, but totally practical, fact that you must plan to be close to home earlier than you actually need to be, in order to cater for delays or problems which could otherwise ruin a marvellous holiday.

DEPARTURE CHECK LIST

- ☐Fresh water?
- ☐Fuel?
- ☐Engine checks?
- ☐Seacocks?
- ☐Weather forecast?
- ☐All loose gear stowed?
- ☐Navigation lights working?
- ☐Pre-cooked food?
- ☐Passage plan?
- ☐Watch system?
- ☐Sails bent on ready?
- ☐Radio check?
- ☐Toys and books ready?
- ☐Anti-seasickness precautions?
- ☐Deck watch properly clothed?
- ☐Harnesses ready?

To summarise the essentials of cruise planning: gather as much information as you can and plan the beginning and end of the cruise. The formal tools are charts, a nautical almanac and books of local information called sailing directions or pilots (coast pilots), but we augment these by magazine articles, local tourist information brochures and knowledge gleaned from friends who have visited the proposed area before. That local knowledge tells you the things which no written guide can – how good the showers are, whether the local pub has a children's room and so on.

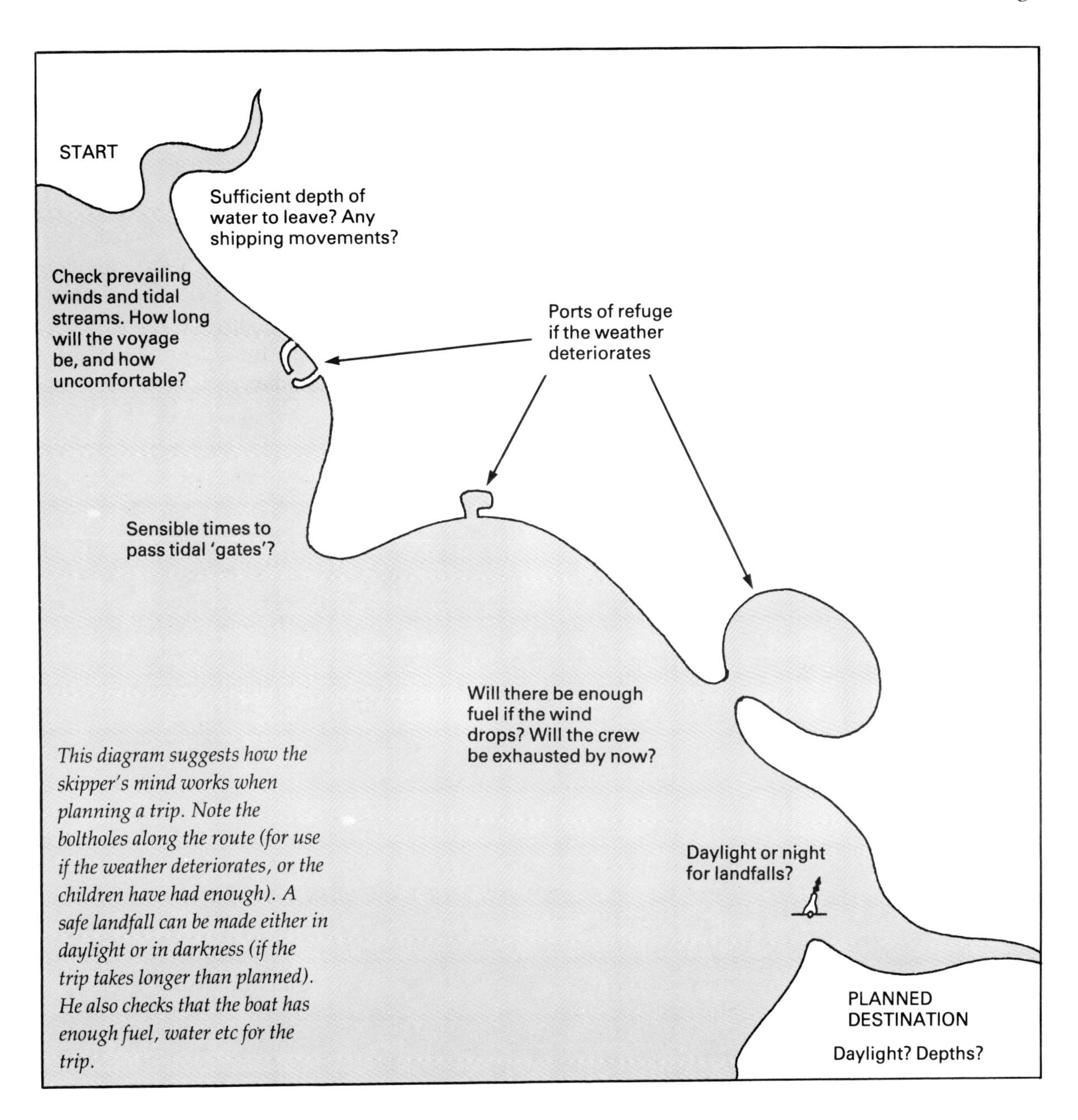

This diagram suggests how the skipper's mind works when planning a trip. Note the boltholes along the route (for use if the weather deteriorates, or the children have had enough). A safe landfall can be made either in daylight or in darkness (if the trip takes longer than planned). He also checks that the boat has enough fuel, water etc for the trip.

The same motto of 'Be prepared' applies particularly to your arrival at a strange place. Bearing in mind that a family cruising with small children is effectively cruising short-handed, think through each stage of your arrival well in advance. If, for example, you are negotiating a complicated estuary, build up a good mental picture of it and don't be afraid to simplify the charted route with an accurate sketch.

If you are going to enter a marina, don't feel coy about calling them up first on VHF to establish where you will be berthed and on which side, so that you can prepare warps and fenders well in advance to avoid last-minute panics. Older children will be helping at this stage (although I have yet to see a father actually hand over the wheel) and even young ones should be involved, even if they only identify buoys or berth numbers.

Do make sure that little ones have been to the heads in the last stages of the passage, so that your attention is not distracted in the middle of a mooring manœuvre by a desperate cry for help.

Arriving at a strange harbour after a successful passage should be a highlight of any cruise, so try to make sure that all the family are involved. Although there might be occasions when you want young children out of the way, we have never had to send ours down below when entering harbour. I attribute that to a spot of pre-planning and clear briefing.

7. *Victualling*

With careful planning and preparation before you set off, victualling need not be a problem. But the less work you do beforehand, the more time you will spend down below making meals when you too could be appreciating the fun and excitement of sailing into a new harbour. A well-stocked larder containing unperishable food means there will be no problem if bad weather delays you or if you want to anchor in a quiet spot and are unable to reach a shop.

Below: Plenty of food at regular intervals will keep the crew happy – but keep it simple and quick to prepare.

Pre-planning

Planning what and how much to take is your main concern. The lack of a fridge will limit the amount of fresh food that you can take. Obviously, what you take depends on the likes and dislikes of your family, but plenty of easily-reached snack foods are always popular such as cheese, crisps, biscuits, fresh and dried fruit, and soft drinks. Soups are always welcome, canned meats and fish a good standby; pasta and rice are quick to cook and very filling. You will also need plenty of longlife juice and milk.

Babies

Breast-feeding on board presents few problems apart from the cold!

Water can be boiled for bottles in the same way as you would at home, and the steriliser taken along. Disposable bottles are available, which are worth considering.

If you usually make up food from packets for a baby who has just started solid food boil the water and keep it in a vacuum flask, ready to prepare on demand. A seat strapped on to the boat, either on or below deck, is a great substitute for a high chair.

Toddlers

Most childen are adaptable and are happy to make a snack of healthy food when they are hungry. A seat that attaches to the saloon table helps them enjoy the meal with the rest of the family.

On short cruises I would not attempt to cook a Sunday roast with two vegetables, as I feel that I am there for the fun as well. Shepherd's pie, fish fingers, chops, bacon, spaghetti bolognese, sausages, cheese on toast, various pasta dishes and eggs are all easy and quick to prepare for children. Anything that requires longer cooking, such as a stew, is better prepared at home and taken to the boat for heating through. Not only is this better for the cook but it also saves on fuel.

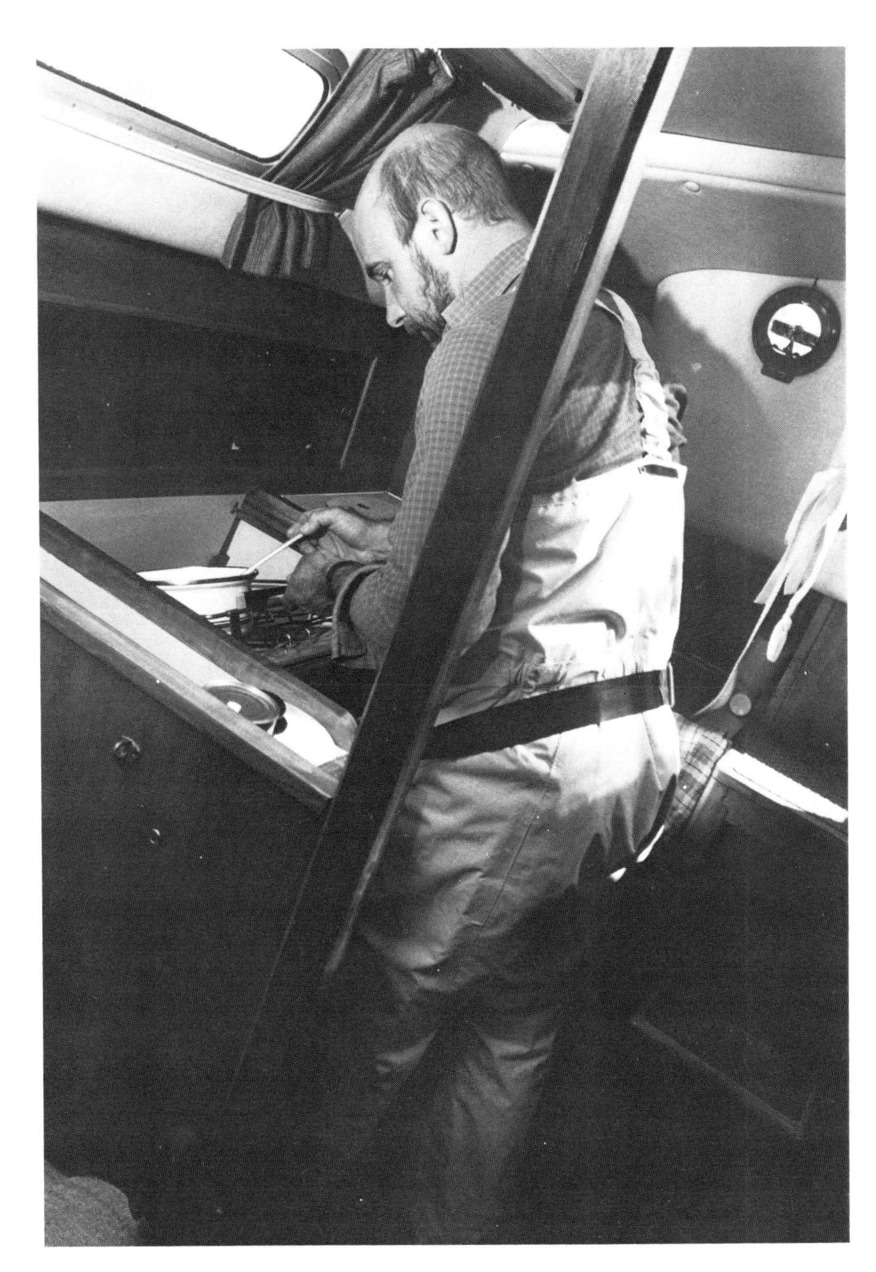

Left: Always wear oilskin trousers when cooking underway. The galley strap provides hands-free security, while a stout bar in front of the stove prevents the cook pitching forward into the soup if the boat rolls.

Eating underway

Hot food can spill all too easily on a passage, so half-fill mugs of hot liquid and use bowls rather than plates.

If your cruising consists of more than short hops from harbour to harbour, you'll find that a pressure cooker is invaluable. Quite apart from the fact that it reduces cooking times, its great advantage aboard is that, no matter what is happening on deck, the meal is cooking safely on the stove. Food doesn't slop about and even if the whole pressure cooker comes off during an unexpected broach, the contents will still be secure. Most food can be cooked in it with careful reference to a good cookbook.

Remember, pre-plan as much as possible, stock up on unperishable goods and use the time you save in the galley to enjoy the sailing.

Recipes

I have detailed below some recipes from June Raper's excellent *Beaufort Scale Cookbook*. These may give inspiration when plain fish fingers fail to excite!

A NOTE ON THE RECIPES
These recipes use imperial and metric measurements. The following abbreviations are used:

lb = pounds
oz = ounces
pt = pint = 2½ (US) cups of liquid

HASTY AND HEARTY

Wind Force 7 — Serves 4

Preparation and cooking time: 10 minutes

12 oz (340g) can corned beef
10 oz (295g) can concentrated tomato soup
9 oz (250g) can rice (or pre-cooked rice)
15¾ oz (447g) can baked beans
7 oz (175g) can tomatoes
large pinch curry powder
seasoning to taste

Break up beef and drain tomatoes. Put all the ingredients except rice into a pan. Heat thoroughly, stirring gently all the time. Add rice and heat through.

This may be served with potato instead of rice.

Remember that tomatoes have been known to make people feel queasy in bad weather. When planning to have this dish, check with the crew.

CHEOY LIN MINCE

Wind Force 6 — Serves 4

Preparation and cooking time: 30 minutes

1 onion
1 lb (450g) mince (ground meat) or 15 oz (425g) can
2 generous dashes Worcester sauce
1 dessertspoon dried parsley
oil
water
2–3 generous dashes tomato ketchup
3 teaspoons dried mixed herbs
15¾ oz (447g) can baked beans
seasoning to taste

Peel and chop onion. Fry gently in a little oil. Add meat and stir in well. Add all other ingredients except beans. Mix well. Cook slowly, stirring occasionally, for 15–20 minutes if using raw mince, otherwise heat thoroughly. Add more water if mixture is too dry. Add beans, heat and check seasoning.

This recipe can be easily adapted to make cottage pie by topping with mashed potato.

POT ROAST IN A PRESSURE COOKER

Wind Force 3 — Serves 6

Preparation and cooking time: 45 minutes

1 lb (450g) carrots
¾ pt (425ml) stock (broth)
3 teaspoons brown sugar
2½ lb (1¼ kg) topside beef
2 large onions
3 tablespoons oil
flour
seasoning to taste

Wash, peel and slice carrots into rings. Peel and slice onion. Wipe meat and rub a little flour over the surface. Heat oil in pressure cooker, add onion, sprinkle with sugar and fry till transparent. Add meat and fry on all sides. Add carrots, seasoning and stock (broth). Bring to boil. Cover and bring to high pressure. Cook for 20–25 minutes depending on how you like your meat. 25 minutes will give you a little pink in the centre. Release pressure quickly. Serve with potatoes and vegetables.

If more meat is used allow 10 minutes per lb (½kg) extra cooking time.

STIR-FRY LIVER AND BACON

Wind Force 3 — Serves 4

Preparation and cooking time: 15 minutes

2 medium onions
1½ lb (675g) lamb's liver
1 tablespoon oil
½ teaspoon made mustard
8 mushrooms
4 large rashers bacon
2–3 teaspoons soya sauce
1 small can garden peas (or fresh/frozen if available)

Peel and slice onions. Clean and slice mushrooms. Wipe and slice liver thinly. Derind bacon and cut into thin strips. Drain peas. Heat oil, soya sauce and mustard in frying pan. Add onions and stir-fry for 2 minutes. Add liver and fry 2 minutes more. Add bacon and mushrooms, fry 1 minute, stirring and tossing. Add peas and heat through quickly. The liver should be pink inside and very tender.

To stir-fry just means to fry quickly over a high heat while tossing and turning the ingredients the whole time so they do not stick or burn. Because the food is thinly sliced it cooks very quickly. Adding more oil should not be necessary but if the pan looks very dry a little can be poured in.

BOILED HAM

Wind Force 4 — Serves 6

Pressure cooker recipe

Preparation and cooking time: 55 minutes

3 lb (1½ kg) ham
1 onion
6 peppercorns
water

Cover ham with water in the pressure cooker and bring to boil. Drain. Cover again with water. Peel onion, add with peppercorns to the ham. Boil at high pressure for 40 minutes. Release pressure quickly. Drain and serve with boiled potatoes, butter beans and mustard.

CHEESY CHICKEN BAKE

Wind Force 7 – if you are game — Serves 4

Preparation and cooking time: 10 minutes

2 × 7½ oz (190g) cans supreme of chicken
5 oz (125g) can peas (or 2 oz (50g) packet)
7 oz (175g) can sweetcorn
4 oz (100g) cheddar cheese
seasoning to taste
1 large packet potato crisps

Open cans, drain vegetables, put with chicken into a pan and mix well. If using packet peas, pre-cook. Heat slowly, stirring occasionally. Slice cheese. Put hot chicken mixture into grill pan (broiler dish), seasoning to taste. Sprinkle crisps over top, crushing as you go. Lay cheese slices on top of crisps and grill (broil) till cheese has melted.

VIERGE CHICKEN

Wind Force 6 — Serves 4

Preparation and cooking time: 1 hour 35 minutes

Oven necessary

4 large portions chicken
seasoning to taste
2 × 7½ (190g) cans mushrooms
¼ pt cream
2 teaspoons crushed garlic
1 teaspoon paprika
10 oz (295g) can condensed cream of chicken soup

Wipe chicken portions. Mix garlic, seasoning and paprika. Rub this spice mixture into chicken. Place in baking dish. Drain mushrooms and sprinkle on top of chicken. Dilute the soup with the cream. Pour over chicken. Bake, uncovered (or loosely covered with foil in bad weather – allowing a small steam vent) in moderately slow oven (300°F/150°C/Gas Mark 2) for 1–1½ hours, till tender.

TOMATO SAUCE FOR SPAGHETTI

Wind Force 4 — Serves 4

Preparation and cooking time: 40 minutes

1 tablespoon oil
1 onion
1 lb (450g) tomatoes
½ teaspoon curry powder
seasoning to taste
1 clove garlic
pinch dried basil
sugar (optional)

Peel and chop tomatoes, onion and garlic. Fry onion and garlic with curry powder in the oil till soft. When the onion mixture is ready, add tomatoes, basil and seasoning. Simmer for 30 minutes. In rough weather, clamp pan to stove and cover with lid or foil with a small steam vent in it. Add a little sugar if desired.

Meanwhile cook spaghetti, drain, pour hot sauce over and serve with Parmesan cheese sprinkled over it.

If the weather permits the dish will be better if you skin the tomatoes before cooking but no harm will come if you leave them on.

FELLOWSHIP FISH FINGERS

Wind Force 4 — Serves 4

Preparation and cooking time:
25 minutes (stove method)
35 minutes (oven method)

6 oz (150g) cheddar cheese
1 tablespoon oil
10 oz (295g) can condensed celery soup
½ teaspoon paprika
1 tablespoon milk
1 small onion
2 large packets fish fingers
seasoning to taste

Stove method

Grate or chop cheese finely. Peel and slice onion finely. Fry onion in oil for 3 minutes. Add fish fingers and fry 5 minutes, turning. Keep hot. In a pan, heat soup, paprika, milk and cheese, reserving a little cheese for top. Season to taste. Pour the mixture over the fish fingers and onion. Sprinkle with remainder of the cheese and grill (broil) for a moment until it melts.

Oven method

Grate or chop cheese finely. Peel and slice onion finely. Lay fish fingers in a lightly greased dish. Mix together cheese, soup, milk, paprika and onion, reserving a little cheese for the top. Season lightly and pour over the fish fingers. Sprinkle grated cheese over. Bake in a moderate oven (350°F/175°C/Gas Mark 4) for about half an hour.

DAVID'S FORCE EIGHT BREAKFAST

Wind Force 8 — Serves 1 (each to his own)

Preparation time: 5 minutes

bacon and eggs as required
2 slices bread

Cut bacon into small pieces with scissors. Drop into deep pan. Fry till soft, shaking occasionally. Add egg(s) to taste. When cooked slide onto slice of bread, top with second slice and eat.

SCRAMBLED EGG IN A BUN

Wind Force 5 — Serves 1

Preparation and cooking time: 10 minutes

1 bun
2 eggs
1 tablespoon milk
1 oz (25g) sharp cheese
seasoning to taste

Grate the cheese with a potato peeler. In a non-stick pan (if possible) mix together well eggs, milk and seasoning. Cook slowly on a low heat, gradually adding cheese and allowing it to melt. As soon as eggs start to set remove from heat and spoon over base of bun. Place lid of bun on top and serve at once.

BACON SANDWICH

Wind Force 6 — Serves 1

Preparation and cooking time: 5 minutes

2 slices bread
bacon or ham rashers
1 egg (optional)

Toast two slices of bread and leave in grill pan (broiler dish). Dry fry bacon or ham rashers. Use bacon fat, if enough, to butter the toast. Place rashers between toast slices. A lightly whipped egg may be fried and added if weather permits.

FRENCH TOAST

Wind Force 5 — Serves 1

Preparation and cooking time: 5 minutes

1 egg
1 slice bread
seasoning to taste
oil

In deep dish break egg up with fork. Add seasoning and whip lightly. Dip both sides of bread (thin slices are best) into egg, soaking liberally. Fry bread quickly in a little oil, pouring in the extra egg as you turn the bread over to fry the other side.

A touch of mustard or dried herbs may be added before cooking. When cooked, cinnamon and sugar or honey may be added.

TARTED UP SEMOLINA

Serves 2

Preparation and cooking time: 8 minutes

1 oz (25g) butter
2 oz (50g) raisins
16 oz (450g) can semolina
1 oz (25g) ground almonds
½ teaspoon cinnamon
2 tablespoons soft brown sugar

Heat butter and add ground almonds, raisins and spice. Cook, stirring, for about 2 minutes. Stir in semolina and allow to heat through. Pour into dish, sprinkle with sugar and flash grill (broil) for 1 minute.

INSTANT TRIFLE

Serves 4

Preparation time: 5 minutes

4 thick slices swiss roll or stale cake
4 tablespoons sherry (adult version only!)
1 can ready made custard
7½ oz (190g) can fruit to suit
10 oz (295g) can cream
chocolate shavings (optional)
nibbed nuts (optional)

In individual bowls place 1 slice swiss roll. Pour a tablespoon of sherry over each. Spoon over some fruit and a little juice to moisten. Divide the can of custard between each dish. Add the cream and smooth over. Sprinkle on some chocolate shavings or nibbed nuts, if desired, and serve.

PEACHY IDEAS

1 can peach halves, or fresh peaches, skinned (2 halves per person)
whipped cream
soft brown sugar

Lay peach halves on flat dish, top with whipped cream and soft brown sugar. Place under grill (broiler) for a moment or two only.

8. *Overboard!*

Losing someone overboard is probably the most frightening experience that is likely to happen to you, but by taking the proper precautions you can remove the risk completely. Prevention is better than cure. If the whole crew remain attached to the yacht, they cannot be lost overboard, even if they miss their footing. The best way of being safe is to keep to a strict discipline about wearing harnesses on deck at sea.

Below: If you make sure everyone stays clipped on to the boat at sea the chances of losing someone overboard are drastically reduced.

Experienced offshore crews often adopt such a routine only when sailing in rough weather or at night, but the couple sailing with children are much more vulnerable, as one parent is often dealing with the children. This leaves the other adult effectively sailing single-handed, which makes every task more time-consuming and more difficult.

However well-intentioned you are, there is always an outside chance that something will go wrong. Your husband leaps up on deck to free a fouled genoa sheet, it clears quickly, flicks him over the side and, before you know it, you have sailed past him. What do you do next?

Basic routine

Below: The first stages in picking up a man overboard. Throw out a lifebuoy, check the children and take the helm (1); then reach off (2) and tack round as soon as you have gained complete control of the boat (3).

1. Immediately throw out a lifebuoy. If he can reach it, it will help to keep him afloat. Even if he can't, it will act as a marker to show his approximate position.

2. Ensure the children are safe. Even if they are too young to help sail the boat, they can still act as extra pairs of eyes to keep sight of the person in the water. Believe me, at sea you very quickly lose sight of a head among the waves.

1

2

3

3. Turn the yacht onto an apparent beam reach, that is to say with the wind blowing directly across the side of the boat – your burgee or wind indicator will be at 90° to your course.

4. Once you have full control of the boat, tack round and return on the other apparent beam reach until you regain sight of the person in the water, probably on your weather bow. Now comes the tricky part. Make your final approach on a close reach, easing the sheets out to control your speed. Aim to stop alongside the person, so that you can throw him a line to establish the vital first contact.

Below: Return on the other reach, sailing back down your track (4); when you see the person in the water luff up to a close reach (5) and ease the sheets to slow the boat as you get ready to help the casualty out of the water (6).

4

5

6

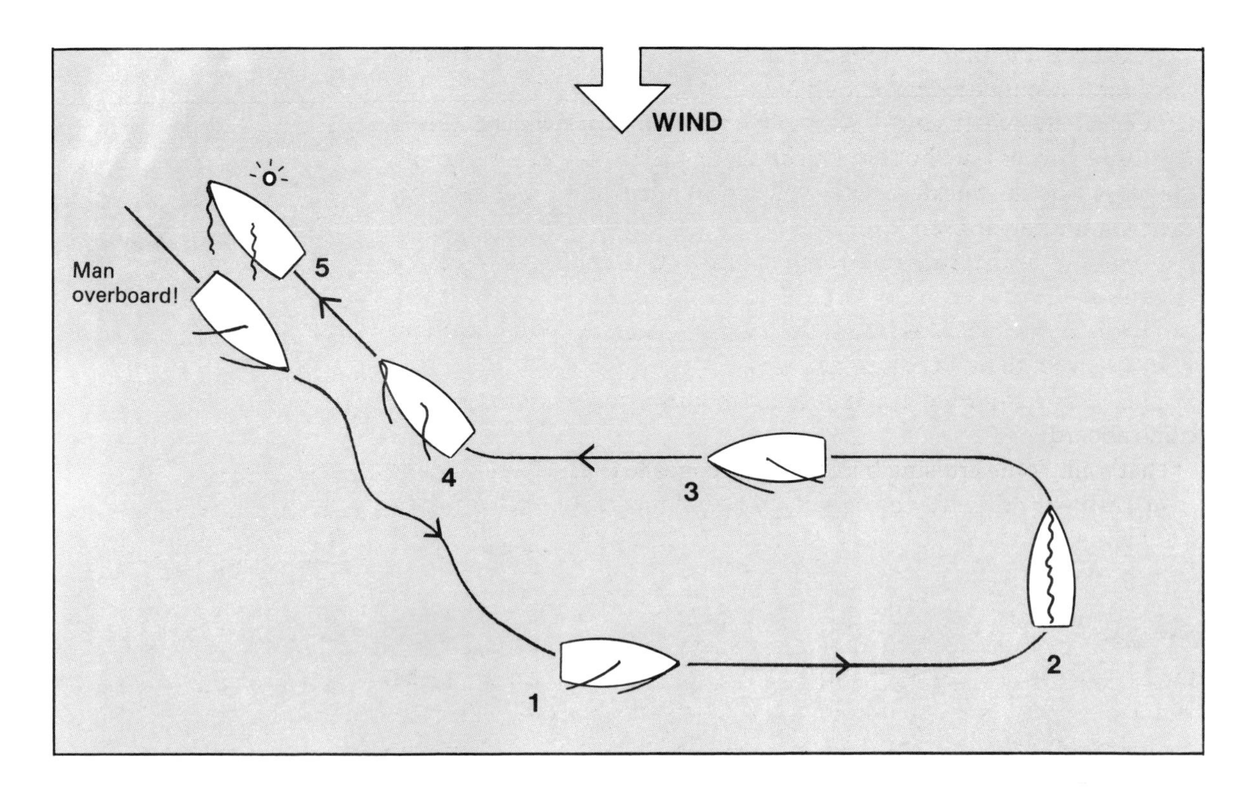

Above: The 'man overboard' drill – reach off (1), tack (2), reach back (3), turn on to a close reach (4) and ease sheets to slow down for the pick-up (5).

GETTING HIM BACK ABOARD

As it is virtually impossible for a swimmer to climb aboard a yacht in a calm anchorage, a man overboard will need help. Assuming that your first contact is made with the heaving line kept ready on the stern pulpit for just such an emergency, you now need to keep him alongside for long enough to prepare the necessary gear.

Keep the boat stopped in the water, either by heaving to or by dropping the genoa and possibly the mainsail too. If you have a fixed or portable boarding ladder, the next stage is relatively easy. If not, all the other options take time and a great deal of effort. Work quickly, because the longer he is in the water, the less he will be able to help – and here I'm talking about minutes, rather than hours.

Make sure that you (and the children) are clipped on securely, and consider the following realistic options:

1. Get a halyard attached to him and winch him back aboard. If he's wearing a harness (without the lifeline) this will simply mean clipping the halyard to the buckle; if not, he'll need a line tied around his chest to which the halyard can be clipped.

2. Use one of the patented recovery gadgets that makes the same job easier.

3. Launch the inflatable dinghy or even the liferaft for him to climb into, and from there to board the yacht.

4. Make a crude rope ladder from a mooring warp so that he can climb aboard.

That's all. Some cruising books devote pages to detailed methods of man overboard recovery using sails lashed along the toe-rail and then rolling the person in but trials at sea, even with fully crewed yachts, have proved unsatisfactory.

AFTERCARE

Quite apart from the treatment of any injuries received during the incident or the recovery (my husband received during one exercise more bruises from a pounding hull and flailing sheets than he did from the 'fall'), anyone who has fallen overboard in temperate waters must be treated for shock and possible hypothermia. Get him below, out of wet clothes into dry ones and gradually rewarm him. Do *not* give the patient alcohol, but a warm drink will be welcome if he's conscious and coherent.

Action in distress

If the unthinkable happens and you cannot find the man overboard, or you have found him but cannot get him back aboard, you need outside help.

Until recently, you were not allowed to use the internationally recognised distress signals if there was only one person in trouble, as they were restricted to times when the whole vessel was 'in grave and imminent danger'.

Thankfully, the position has now changed, and man overboard is one of the categories that justify the use of a VHF Mayday message or distress flares. Although you might have been to evening classes or read other cruising books which list the fourteen internationally recognised means of indicating that you are in distress, these two are the only ones that are any use to you on a yacht. You can forget about all the others.

Using a VHF radiotelephone is no more difficult than using the phone at home, provided you remember a few basic principles. If you are familiar with VHF procedures, because you have used it for routine calls to harbour masters, other yachts or for link calls to the shore, you won't be in such a panic if you have to make a distress call.

The best course of action is to learn the full VHF procedure. (In Britain you can take a short exam for a Certificate of Competence.)

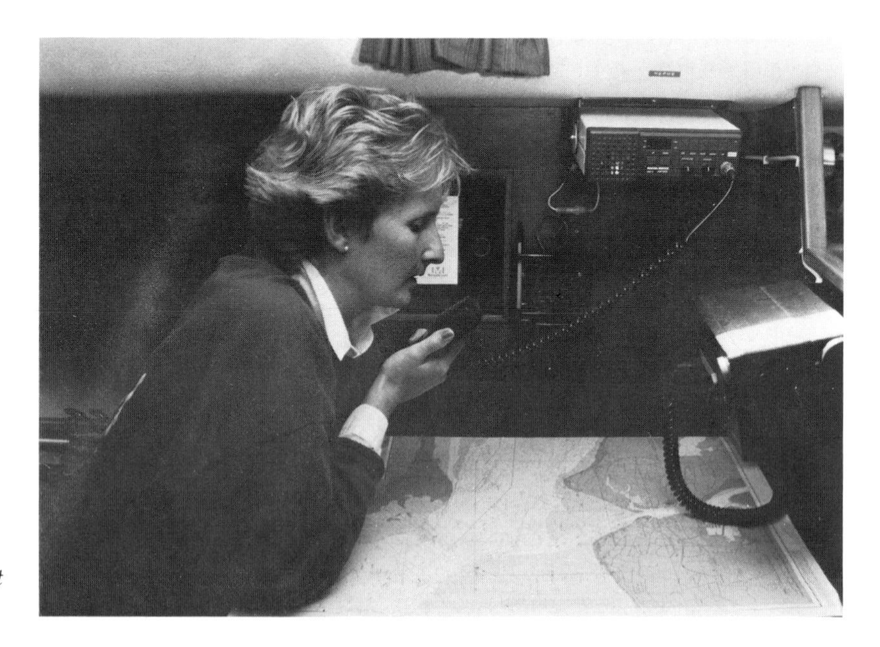

Right: Make sure you are familiar with the VHF set by using it to talk to other boats or land stations. In an emergency it could be your only lifeline.

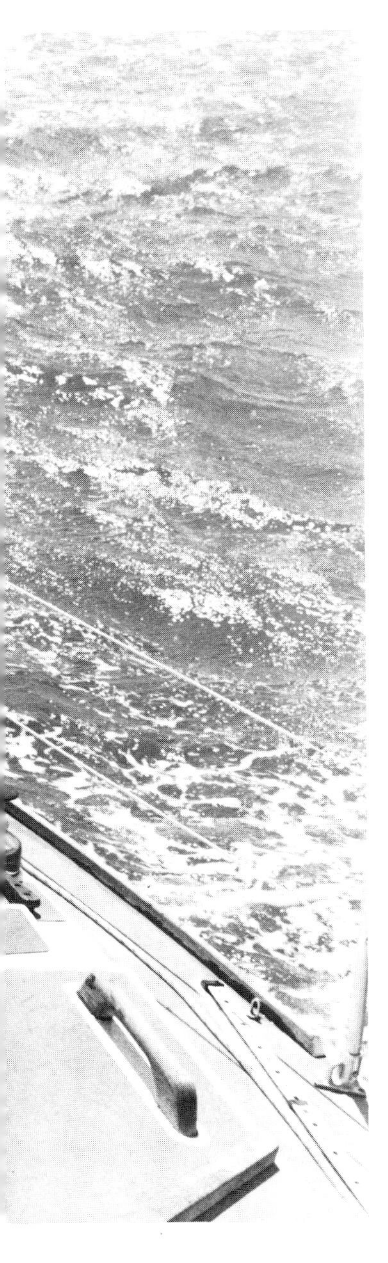

3. *Mental Attitude*

Enthusiasm is the key to enjoyment of most sports, and sailing is no exception.

The mere fact that all the family can take part together makes sailing unusual. The very nature of cruising means that household distractions and chores are left behind, allowing the family to work and play together in a tightly-knit group where everyone's needs and feelings are important.

Any challenging passage planned and made is an achievement for the whole family, regardless of its length or the time it takes. Whether it is merely crossing an estuary or crossing the Channel, success relies on the enjoyment and participation of the whole crew.

Children are quick to learn but are extremely sensitive to atmosphere, good or bad. In particular, a mother's feelings are very easily transferred to her children. If you are terrified about the safety of your children on board they will become nervous, unsettled and unsure.

If you have taken all the safety precautions that you feel are necessary, an air of quiet confidence should prevail. As long as the child is wearing a harness and is clipped on to the boat he cannot drown. In turn, this gives the child the freedom to enjoy himself, experiment and follow what is going on, thus playing an active role in the sailing.

To attempt long passages with small children is to invite trouble – unless you take certain precautions. To prevent squabbling, the children must be kept well occupied and know that they have the security of their own bunk with their favourite toys as a refuge. Smaller children love drawing, playing 'I-Spy' and listening to

Right: With father below making lunch, and mother looking after the ship, life on board can be something of an eye-opener for a small child.

But even a novice sailor should know how to send a distress call and message. Many yacht owners keep a Mayday crib-sheet ready for an emergency close to the VHF set.

BASIC PROCEDURE FOR A MAYDAY CALL

1. Switch on and select high power (25 watts).

2. Select Channel 16 and wait for silence.

3. Hold the 'Press to Transmit' button and give the following message, using your own boat name and nature of distress:

'Mayday, Mayday, Mayday.
This is Drumbeat, Drumbeat, Drumbeat.
Mayday Drumbeat.
My position is . . . . '
Then give nature of distress and
Any other relevant information
'Over'

4. Release the 'Press to Transmit' button and listen for a response. All subsequent communications will be on Channel 16 and should be prefaced by the word 'Mayday' and your boat name.

The order in which you give the information is logical. The most important part of it is your position. Get that wrong and anyone trying to help will waste valuable time.

There are two accepted methods of giving your position. The first is your latitude and longitude. If your boat is equipped with a Decca Navigator or one of the other hyperbolic or satellite position fixing systems, this is easy, as long as you know which buttons to press to give the information. Alternatively, if you have been keeping up the chartwork, you should be able to read your current latitude and longitude off the chart.

For the majority of people engaged in day sailing or coastal cruising, it is far easier – and more practical – to give your position by the other accepted method: your true bearing and distance *from* a conspicuous object.

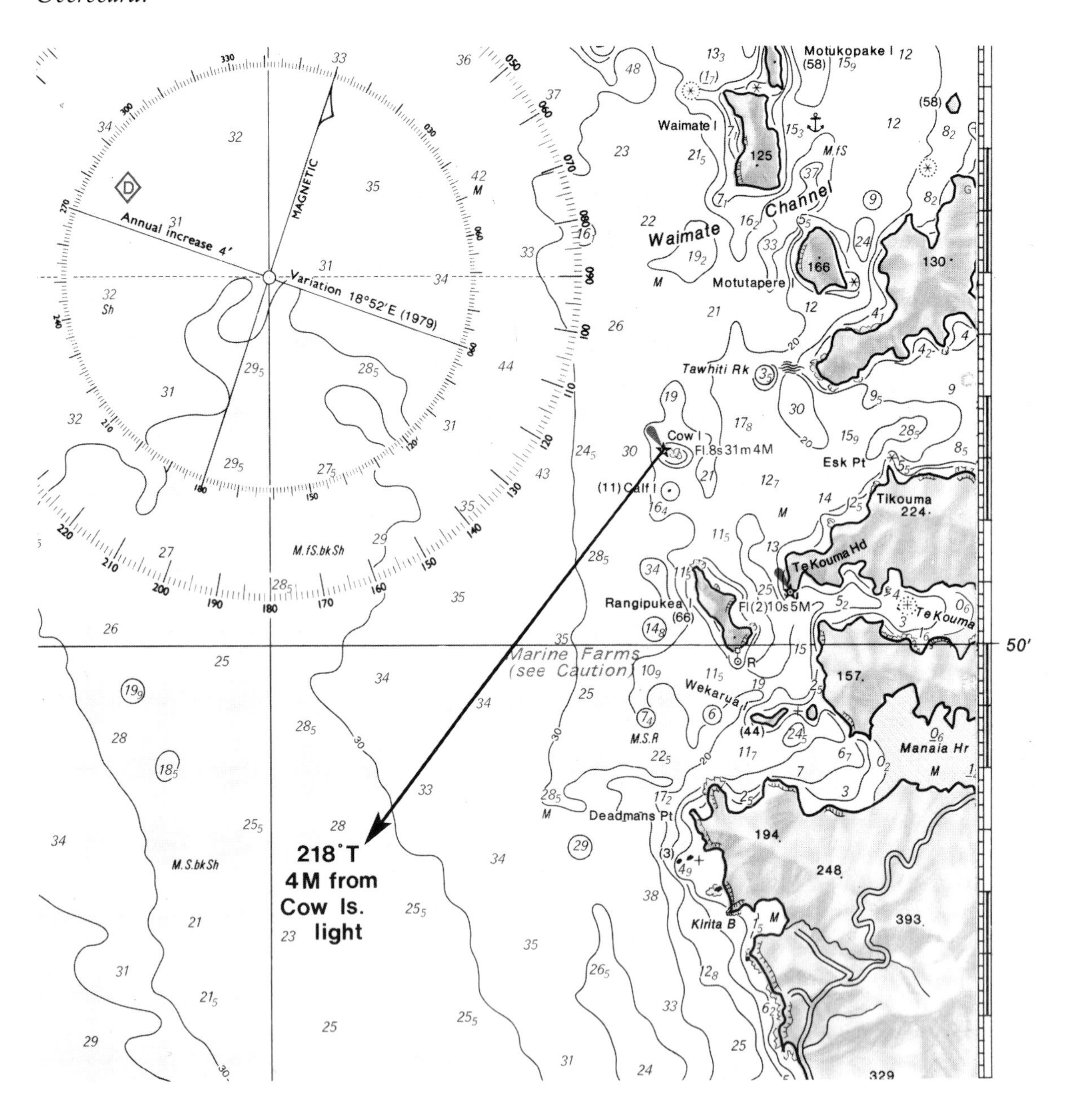
218° T
4 M from
Cow Is.
light
Cow I
Fl.8s 31m 4M
Calf I
Rangipukea I
Fl(2)10s 5M
Waimate Channel
Waimate I
Motukopake I
Motutapere I
Tawhiti Rk
Esk Pt
Tikouma
TeKouma Hd
Te Kouma
Manaia Hr
Wekarua I
Deadmans Pt
Kirita B
Marine Farms
(see Caution)
MAGNETIC
Annual increase 4′
Variation 18°52′E (1979)
50′

Not only is it easier for you immediately to identify your position as, say, 225° true from the Eddystone lighthouse 5 miles, but that gives everyone within radio range an instant mental picture of your location. The crucial parts of the information are that the bearing is *true* (not magnetic) and that you give the bearing *from* the conspicuous object. In that example above, if you had hurriedly taken a compass bearing of the lighthouse and given that as your bearing, any rescuers would have been looking for you ten miles from your actual position, even ignoring the extra error for the magnetic bearing.

For other urgent communications that do not justify the use of a Mayday call and message (which effectively silences all other radio traffic) use the Pan-Pan call. Your message then takes priority over all traffic except distress messages.

The great advantage of VHF over the use of flares is that it provides two-way communication so that the rescue agencies can establish exactly what is wrong and so best decide what help is needed.

Flares

If you don't have a VHF radiotelephone, or if it won't work, you'll have to rely on flares. Once again, familiarity with their operation is important. The time to find out how they work is not at dead of night in the middle of the ocean with your husband lost overboard.

There are essentially two different types of distress flares in common use: parachute flares and hand-held flares.

As the name suggests, parachute flares on the principle of firing a rocket up to a certain height (about 300 m, 1000 ft) after which the flare comes down under a parachute. The great advantage of this type is that the flare can be seen from many miles away, so they are a useful long-distance alert. The disadvantage is that, while a red parachute flare tells others that you are in trouble, it won't pinpoint your position.

That is the job of the hand-held flare, either a pinpoint red flare for

Far left: If you have to make a distress call, make sure you give your position correctly. In this example, the yacht's position is 218 degrees TRUE, 4 miles FROM Cow Island light.

Right: All adults and older children should know WHERE the flares are stowed, WHEN to use the different types and HOW they are operated.

night use or an orange smoke flare for daytime. Neither can be seen for more than a few miles (i.e. the horizon when you are at deck height on a yacht) but they will indicate exactly where you are. Both burn for about a minute, like the parachute flare.

There is another option for daytime use that provides a longer burning time. No yacht flare pack is complete without some buoyant orange smoke flares that, after they have been triggered and thrown over the leeward side of the boat, belch out orange smoke for about three minutes.

Firing mechanisms vary between manufacturers, so the best thing to do is to have a good look at your flare pack on a quiet day when the children aren't around, so that you will know what to do when the occasion arises. If you cruise regularly with different groups of friends, don't think you are scaremongering if you show them where the flares are stowed and how they work when you are showing them around the boat.

If the children are old enough, they they too should be taught how to use flares. Don't go firing off old ones for practice; instead, if you get the opportunity, attend one of the flare demonstrations given at yacht clubs under controlled conditions.

There are two other sorts of flares that you should know about. The first are personal flares, intended to be carried in an oilskin pocket so that if you fall overboard at night you can use them to guide a rescuer to you. The most popular type falls somewhere between the conventional parachute and the hand-held flare. This flare is projected to a much lower height than a parachute flare and only burns for a few seconds, but it does have a greater range than a hand-held flare.

The second is not a distress flare at all, and it is important that you should know the difference. White hand-held flares are often stowed with the distress flares but they should be stowed separately. White flares provide a very bright white light for a limited period. The most common reason for using them is to indicate your position clearly at times when you are not in distress but need to draw attention to yourself. The obvious example is when you think that the crew of a ship have not seen you and are about to run you down!

But don't let all this talk of disasters put you off going cruising. You're much safer at sea than on the road driving down to your boat and, if you take the right precautions, none of the disasters will ever happen.

9. *Keeping Clean and Healthy*

Everyone has their own standard of cleanliness, and mothers with small children are all aware of the importance of hygiene. It is not easy to keep the children spotlessly clean at all times while cruising, though. Be prepared to relax your standards when the family has been helping to wash the boat down following a muddy walk in their wellington boots.

Washing and bathing

In most popular family cruising areas, water is plentiful. A quick wash with a flannel and some warm soapy water can be a lot of fun, particularly if the children are allowed to do it themselves on deck where nobody is troubled if water is spilt.

Most marinas have showers for the use of visiting yachtsmen – but have you ever tried sharing one with a three-year-old? It is difficult to run after them if they manage to escape through the soggy shower curtain and even harder to catch them if they are covered in soap. The best technique is to use just enough water to wet the child. Turn off the shower and concentrate on getting soap where it is most needed. Then turn on the shower again to rinse everything off.

Many boats now have showers on board, which is a wonderful luxury to the mother with small children – even if she just uses it to boost her own morale and wash her hair! Incidentally, the technique described above can be used aboard to save water, so that there is no squabbling about who gets a shower and who doesn't. However, since yacht hot water systems usually draw water from a calorifier run via the engine cooling system, you might have to plan ahead, as the engine has to be run to heat the water before the shower is used.

A small baby or toddler can be 'topped and tailed' very effectively. Interspersed with a shower every now and again, this is perfectly adequate during a family cruise.

Washing clothes

Family cruising boats can be easily spotted in a marina as they are the ones with a permanent display of small clothes hanging on a washing line. (It can also discourage people from mooring alongside when they realise there are children on board!)

In much the same way that single-handed sailors are identified by the self-steering gear on the stern, you can always tell the families

Left: A 'spider' clothes drier and a few lengths of shock cord provide very adequate drying facilities and are easily stowed away when not needed.

who are serious about their cruising – they are the ones with the clever 'spider' clothes dryers which fold down into almost nothing for stowage.

There are plenty of travel-sized washing soaps on the market that are ideal to keep on board and I would suggest that you make use of a spell of reasonable weather to catch up on a little washing that can be left to dry while the family take a trip ashore – it is a lot less trouble than a panic wash when everything is dirty. If you wait till then, you can be sure that the weather will be awful, leaving you trying to get everything dry below deck.

Some marinas now have launderettes with drying facilities, and you can usually find advertisements for local laundries that will collect your washing and return it, beautifully laundered . . . for a small fee.

First Aid

Every yacht should carry a comprehensive First Aid kit, with any additions needed for a particular crew. It is important, however, to separate your family's pills, tablets and creams from the First Aid kit proper, which will largely consist of dressings and bandages.

Although you can buy ready-made kits at chemists and chandlers, we prefer to make up our own with more large dressings and bandages than the minimum usually supplied. We work on the basis that even minor wounds can take on more significance if you are offshore with a young crew. Plastic ice cream containers, suitably labelled, serve to keep everything dry and in one place.

We were very grateful for an adequate First Aid kit soon after buying one boat when our two-year-old daughter fell off the forward bunk, splitting her head open on the main bulkhead. It was a very cold winter's day but fortunately, far from being offshore, we were in the marina with the car at the end of the pontoon and within a short drive of the local hospital.

That episode reminded us that when you lay a boat up for the winter, one thing you don't take home for storage in the loft is the First Aid kit. It is also essential that the kit is in an accessible place, which is another good reason for separating it from the pills and potions of the medicine chest.

Remember that medicines should be out of the reach of small children; the same rules apply afloat as in the home. The classic stand-bys like Calpol and children's aspirin will be needed, together with creams or sprays for insect stings and something for the most common cruising ailments of seasickness and sunburn.

SUGGESTED MINIMUM FIRST AID KIT

10 individually wrapped sterile dressings	3 medium sized sterile dressings
1 sterile eye pad	1 large sterile dressing
1 triangular bandage	1 extra-large sterile dressing
1 sterile covering for serious wound	cotton wool
6 safety pins	scissors
	tweezers

Seasickness

Following one unforgettable passage back across the Channel that I put down more to bad *moules* in Cherbourg rather than rough weather, I got to grips early in my cruising career by sailing with a couple of doctor friends who were just developing a new remedy for seasickness. Knowing that motion sickness was caused by the balance mechanism located in the ears, they conducted a whole series of trials and eventually persuaded one of the pharmaceutical giants to market for seasickness a drug previously used for ear/balance disorders.

The drug is commercially known as Stugeron (Cinnarizine), and it's fair to say that it has caused a quiet revolution for weekend cruising folk. While it has helped many yachtsmen get over the trauma of the first couple of days at sea, it doesn't help everyone and there may be complications. If you are pregnant, for example, or receiving any kind of medication, do consult your doctor about possible side effects.

On the same subject, we heard from one friend who was more than usually seasick during one week's cruise. On returning home she had her suspicions confirmed by a positive pregnancy test! If you use the contraceptive pill and are sick, the pill's effectiveness may be reduced and you should take extra precautions.

Anti-seasickness tablets allow parents and older children to carry on as normal, but we have heard from several yachtsmen, worried about side- and after-effects, who say they would never use any anti-seasickness tablets for their children. Instead, they rely on providing plenty of fluid and dry biscuits.

The most common side-effects of Stugeron are initial drowsiness (which can be overcome by starting the course of tablets a couple of days before going afloat, so that you're tired at home, rather than at sea) and you are more likely to suffer from land-sickness on coming ashore after a long passage. The latter wears off fairly quickly, but it's safest to plan your cruise so you don't have to drive home immediately after coming ashore from a long passage.

If any of your crew are feeling sick, there are two possible remedies. The first is to get the affected person to steer the boat. Concentrating on a task and keeping his eyes on the horizon may have the necessary settling effect on the helmsman.

The alternative, much as it may be unpopular, is to get the victim down below and into a bunk, with instructions to sleep. The receptors in the ear that cause the trouble switch off when the head is horizontal. It's not always foolproof. During one memorable passage in the Channel Islands – a twenty-five-mile beat into a Force 5–6 – I was steering when I heard a plaintive call from my son, aged five, 'Mummy, Charlotte's coughing.' Charlotte wasn't exactly coughing, but as I didn't feel too good it was my husband who had to clear up the mess down below.

If you have a seasick crew on deck, there is only one place for them to be – sitting on the leeward side of the boat, properly dressed for the weather conditions and securely harnessed on. If your crew includes

Left: Taking over the helm will often cure any queasiness; many quite small children can steer a boat effectively provided they can see over the coachroof.

the in-laws, it may be worth reminding them to remove their false teeth if they are feeling really ill.

Too much sun

We all know that the effects of the sun are heightened at sea (after all, that's one of the reasons we go afloat, isn't it?) The real problem is not the scorching hot days when we take precautions anyway but those typical summer days with a mixture of sun, cloud and wind, when we may underestimate the power of the sun.

Protection is better than cure so arm yourself with whatever creams your family needs, ranging through to total sun block and not forgetting the after-sun moisturiser. You are less likely to have problems with sunburnt children when you are at sea than on days spent in harbour, because then most of the vulnerable areas, apart from faces, are likely to be covered.

During hot, calm days spent at anchor or in harbour, you might need to rig some sort of shade over the cockit, as children may be reluctant to go below into a stuffy cabin. If you don't have a purpose-made boom tent, a sail does a perfectly adequate job; indeed it might be the only time you'll use the storm jib . . . if you're lucky!

The value of tee shirts and sun-hats in protecting pale parts of the anatomy is just as great as on any holiday. In addition, learn the signs of impending heat exhaustion: the casualty may feel exhausted but restless and may have a headache and feel sick (it is difficult to disassociate this from seasickness, though). The most obvious signs are that, even though the weather is hot, the casualty looks pale, with a cold and clammy skin. Breathing becomes fast and shallow and the pulse is rapid and weak.

The treatment is to get the casualty out of the heat, so take him below and get him into a bunk. Sips of cold water help and, in severe cases, when the casualty has cramps, diarrhoea or is sick, give him lightly salted water. Don't over do this or you could make the nausea worse. About half a teaspoon of salt per half-litre (pint) of water is right. You can disguise the taste with orange juice.

This is just one of the things you would learn on a First Aid course, which is useful preparation for the other minor calamities which might befall you when cruising with children. In our experience, apart from the inevitable bumps and scrapes which are part of childhood, the greatest risk comes from burns and scalds.

Small children, who at home cannot reach the hot danger areas of a domestic cooker, find it easy to climb onto a settee berth and poke enquiring fingers into the flame of a yacht cooker. Similarly, splashes from hot liquids are less easily controlled at sea than at home. Follow a strict regime when cooking with small children aboard.

If older children are involved in the preparation of hot food or drinks at sea, they must be shown, preferably by example, the good practice of wearing oilskin trousers when cooking. Together with the usual rule of not trying to fill mugs or bowls too full, this helps to overcome both spillages and their effects.

Baby needs

In many ways babies are less trouble when cruising than toddlers. Your favourite brand of disposable nappies (diapers) will take up a good deal of stowage space, together with plenty of plastic bags so that the soiled nappies can be double wrapped before going into the rubbish bin at the next port of call.

The 'travelling' sort of changing mat is a great asset. It allows the parent to keep wipes, powder, creams and replacement nappies together in one place and so get the job done quickly – vital at sea if you're not feeling well in the first place.

Don't let that thought put you off, though, any more than you would be dissuaded from travelling anywhere else with a baby.

10. *Onboard Entertainment*

Keeping children entertained afloat can be one of the hardest parts of your cruising. Let's face it, some passages can be boring enough for adults, let alone lively children who don't want to be cooped up on board.

As I've said earlier, the best way to tackle the problem is to keep offshore passages as short as practical, or make them at night. Failing that, other answers are outlined below, according to the children's ages.

Up to eight months

The best entertainment for babies is to be involved in everything that's going on around them. A popular way to do this is to use an infant's car seat, suitably mounted, perhaps bolted to the stern pulpit.

A more common alternative, which keeps baby rather better protected, is to make up a special spare washboard (hatchboard) for the main hatch, with the seat bolted to that. The only disadvantage is that, like the 'house' which our children create, it restricts access below.

Another idea is to mount the car seat below, secured to the back of a settee berth, with a range of hanging toys. At sea the motion ensures that mobiles really live up to their name! Children of this age spend a lot of the time asleep, particularly if lulled by the sound of waves lapping gently against the side of the boat.

In harbour, try hanging a baby bouncer from the boom over the cockpit. It's quite entertaining for the crews of nearby boats, as well as interesting for the child.

Nine to eighteen months

Until the child starts to walk with any confidence, the best place to be is secure in a bunk which has a proper leeboard (see Chapter 5). There's plenty of room to crawl around, the hard corners are well padded with sleeping bags and toys cannot get lost. The really annoying part is when Mummy won't retrieve the toy you've just thrown across the cabin because she's busy helping Daddy with a sail change or picking up a mooring.

As soon as the cruising child masters walking, the next thing to learn is how to clip on the safety harness. There's usually plenty going on to occupy little ones of this age, secure in the cockpit.

Left: The simplest toys will often keep the children occupied while you concentrate on a tricky mooring manoeuvre.

Eighteen months to three years old

Below: Keep a good choice of simple activities ready for when boredom sets in on a long passage. Drawing and colouring are always useful standbys.

This is the time when the boat seems to be filled with crayons, sticky shapes and pieces of paper covered in various forms of art. There's no shortage of inspiration: the child can draw what he sees immediately in view or his memories of the previous port. When that gets boring, there's always noughts and crosses or even 'I-Spy' to occupy young minds.

Left: Fishing or crabbing provides hours of entertainment in harbour, but seems to lose its attraction more quickly when underway.

In harbour, fishing starts to take up a lot of time, regardless of the fact that the fishing line might be as thick as a spare warp or sheet. Once they progress to fishing with those little nets most often used for sticklebacks or tadpoles on the local pond, do make sure that you have something to hand ready to retrieve the net when it is dropped over the side.

Crabbing is also great fun: tie a paperclip to the end of a line and impale a piece of bacon on the paperclip. Let the bacon sink to the bottom, wait, then raise it gently to see if there's a crab on the end.

No family yacht is fully equipped unless it carries a mackerel line for each small crew member, even though it is probably Dad who has to get it streamed in the first place and then deal with anything caught.

Other essential pieces of yacht equipment for this age group are buckets, spades and a football for the beach stops (which should be as frequent as possible). You will also need plastic bags for the shell collections made on every beach and then immediately forgotten. If you don't insist on them being kept in a bag, you'll soon find fragments of shell everywhere underfoot on the boat.

Over three years

As children take more of an interest in sailing, they can help with various tasks around the boat, as outlined in the next chapter. They can also play a more active part in planning some aspects of cruising, if you involve them in choosing where you are going, and deciding what provisions you'll need when you get there or where you are going to eat.

This is the time to feed in plenty of information about your next port of call. I'm not talking here about architectural or historical features, but whether there's a McDonalds within walking distance of the quay and whether the local supermarket stays open late on Thursdays.

Children of this age should be taught about the problems of life at sea. I'll never forget the time we diverted in answer to a distress flare from a small runabout which was sinking. Our crew consisted of my husband, me, two children aged five and three, together with their grandparents. In just the same way that a television 'yottie' drama had earlier impressed upon them the dangers of running on the marina pontoon, so this episode showed them the use and response to flares and the result of someone taking a small boat to sea inadequately prepared for bad weather. It's all very well telling children to wrap up warmly against the cold, but when they see a shivering child, dressed only in a swimming costume and lifejacket

Left: Personal stereos will keep children entertained for hours while you get on with sailing the boat. You can supply them with story tapes as well as music, and these are also far less audible (and less irritating) to others.

(PFD), being rescued from a swamped runabout, the message is remembered.

The over-threes enjoy a wide range of games and entertainments afloat. The travelling versions of popular board games are ideally suited to use on the boat, as long as the playing pieces cannot find their way into the bilge and clog the pump.

Whatever your views on some of the computer 'arcade' games widely sold in toyshops, those dedicated to helping spelling or maths are welcome. If your ideas are more traditional, there are books of crosswords and the old favourites of hangman, dominoes and battleships.

Look out for tablecloths or towels that have games printed on them. Some will only be suitable for calm weather passages or time spent at anchor, but they all add to the battery of onboard entertainment.

Talking of batteries, you'll need a good supply of them. If you opt for rechargeable ones you have to sort out the problem of recharging them from your ship supply.

Below: Although the principles of chartwork may be beyond the understanding of a six-year-old, he can still appreciate the picture that a chart has to offer.

The heaviest battery user of all is the personal stereo. You either love them or hate them; we bought them when the children were five and four, and have never regretted the decision. You can act as Editor

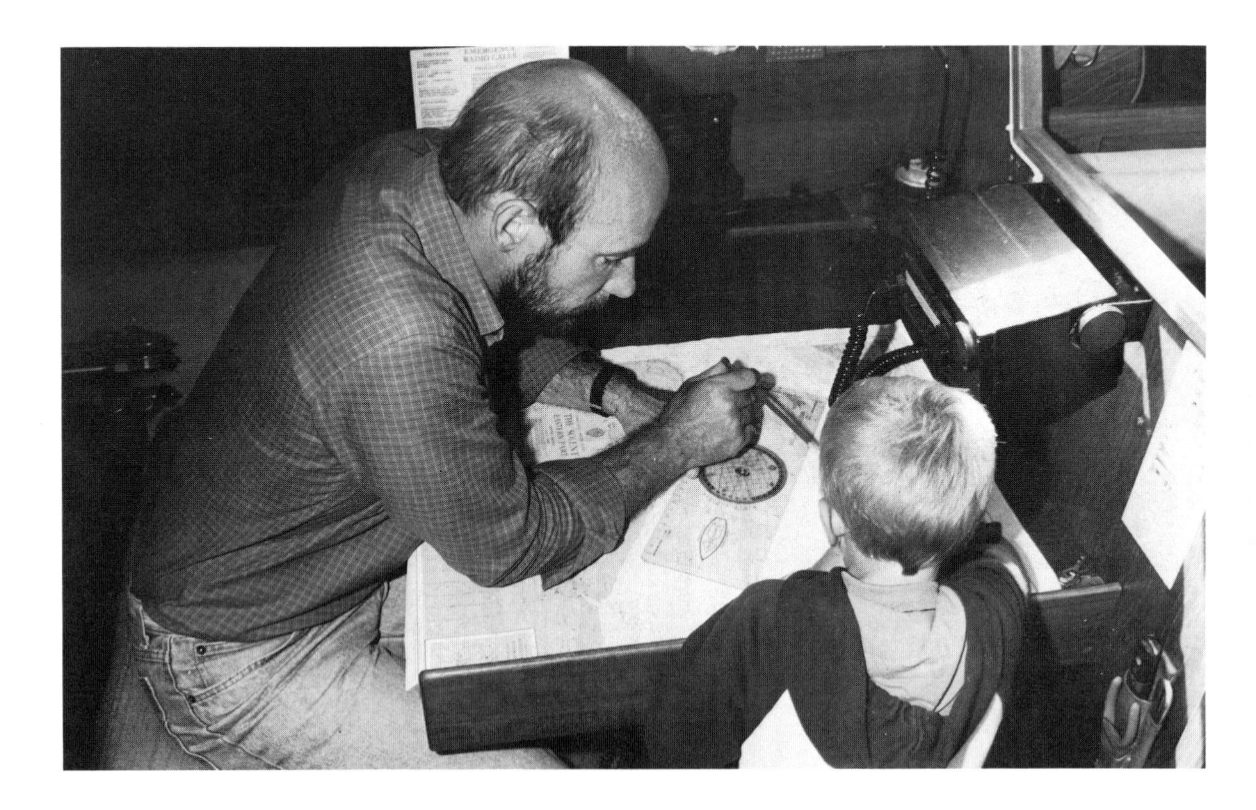

in Chief to ensure that the tapes are suitable. It's sometimes a blessing to know that the children are warm, happy and entertained, while you have some drama to sort out.

Finally, don't ever forget that, while many of the above ideas are merely diversions or distractions, your children have the opportunity to learn so much about the world around them through your cruising. Encourage them to use the chart and a hand bearing compass just as soon as the numbers, words and shapes make sense. If your skipper pales at the idea, because your hand bearing compass isn't one of the indestructible types, invest in a cheap orienteering compass from a camping shop. Buy a few up-to-date charts for the boat, so that the children can have the old ones. The fascination of poring over charts,

Above: Encourage your child to practise using the hand bearing compass. What starts out as a game may finish up being extremely useful when you are dodging the freighters in a shipping lane.

Below: While the navigator is down below the crew on watch can call out log readings and enjoy a sense of involvement.

Right: The ship's binoculars are always in demand – but make sure the strap goes round the wearer's neck first. Binoculars are more delicate than they look, and a sharp knock can leave you seeing double. . . .

looking out for landmarks with a pair of binoculars and plotting your position will keep them going for ages, but watch out for the day when they can work out the next tidal height calculation faster than the skipper!

Five suggested games

FIZZ BUZZ

This is a counting game suitable for any number of players. You start with 1 and count in turn. You must not say the numbers 5 or 7. Instead, say Fizz every time a number containing 5 comes round and Buzz whenever there should be a 7.

For older children (and I must admit for adults on a long passage) you can make the game more difficult by ruling that any numbers which are multiples of 5 or 7 must be replaced by Fizz or Buzz respectively – 35 becomes FizzBuzz.

Get it wrong and you lose a life and start again from 1. Lose three lives and you're out.

HANG THE SKIPPER

This is the nautical version of the old favourite, hangman. One person thinks of a word associated with sailing or the sea and draws a number of blank lines on a piece of paper representing the number of letters in the word.

The other player then has to guess the letters which will fill those spaces. If a letter is correct, the first player puts it on the appropriate space; if not, he starts to draw a hangman. When the hangman is complete, the word setter has won and has another go. If, on the other hand, the other player guesses the word before he has run out of 'lives', he becomes the hangman.

KIM'S GAME

This is a favourite test of observation and memory. Someone (usually Mum or Dad) puts a whole range of different small objects out on a tray, on the chart table or even in a sailbag. The players have a limited time to look at everything and memorise what they see. The objects are then covered up. The winner is the player who can remember the greatest number of objects.

In another version of the game, the objects are covered up and one is removed before they are revealed again. The winner this time is the person who first identifies what is missing.

DAVY JONES'S LOCKER

This is a mental version of Kim's game. One person starts by saying 'In Davy Jones's locker he has a winch handle. . . .' The next person starts in the same way, repeating the first item and adding something else, such as 'In Davy Jones's locker he has a winch handle and a bosun's chair. . . .' Each person carries on in the same way, so that the list gets longer and longer. Anyone who forgets an item is out (and presumably sent down to Davy Jones's locker to look for it!).

BATTLESHIPS

This is another appropriate game for young sailors. Both players have to make up two grids of 10 × 10 squares on a piece of paper, keyed 1–10 along one edge and A–J along the other. They then agree what size fleets they are going to have. It's conventional to have one

1	2	3	4	5	6	7	8	9	10	
	A									A
						F	F			B
B	B	B	B							C
								F		D
			A					F		E
					D	D	D			F
		D							A	G
		D								H
		D		F				A		I
				F						J

A grid for playing battleships with a fleet in position. B = battleship; D = destroyer; F = frigate; A = aircraft.

battleship which takes up four spaces, two destroyers which each take up three spaces, three frigates which each take up two spaces and four aircraft which take up one space each.

Each player places his fleet on his grid by writing a B in four adjoining spaces for the battleship and so on. One player starts firing by calling out the grid reference for a square (e.g. D5). The second player marks the square on his grid with a cross. If that square is occupied by part of a ship, he tells the first player what sort of vessel has been hit and the first player marks the square on his spare grid with the appropriate letter and has another shot. Each time a player misses a target, he stops firing and the other player starts. The winner is the first to destroy all the enemy fleet.

If you are cruising in an area with a naval history, try ringing the changes by substituting galleons, corvettes or fireships for more modern vessels.

11. *Helping and Learning to Sail*

Our crews have included helpless babies, strapping hulks of teenage boys, and all ages in between. Their contribution to family cruising has varied enormously. Our aim is to encourage all our crews, regardless of age, to take as much part in the tasks of sailing and boat handling as they want, knowing that if necessary the boat can be sailed single-handed.

Ironically, with a properly balanced wheel-steered yacht, the first real sailing task that our children and their friends could accomplish was steering. The loads on the wheel are less than those on the sheets and halyards and the sense of achievement for a three-year-old in steering a yacht is immense.

A child has a short concentration span, however, and it probably won't be long before the young child wants to abandon the wheel in favour of his toys, even if you try to make the task more exciting by aiming for buoys, objects on a distant shore and so on.

During short coastal passages you can involve children as look-outs, possibly in the form of 'I-Spy' games but, unless you are lucky enough to be shadowed by dolphins or submarines, this sort of activity doesn't work offshore.

Young children do not possess the physical strength demanded by many of the tasks involved in handling a cruising yacht at sea. There's no way round this problem: for safety's sake, children can only be entrusted with jobs that are within their capabilities. But as they grow older, and stronger, they have the satisfaction of becoming ever more useful members of the crew.

Far left: Who needs parents anyway? Train your children well and you can settle back with a martini while they run the ship.

Entering harbour, it is a different story; there is equipment to stow, fenders to find and put into position, buoys and other boats to spot

PRELUDE
PRELUDE

Right: Encourage the children to help as lookouts by giving them specific landmarks or objects to identify.

and plenty of ropes to tidy. Once the boat is safely moored, there are lots of other jobs which young children can do, or help to do. Washing the decks is a favourite task, together with drying up, helping Dad to do engine checks, filling the water tank, carrying gear or rubbish ashore and a host of others. Then there's the world of the inflatable dinghy and all the excitement and joy it can bring.

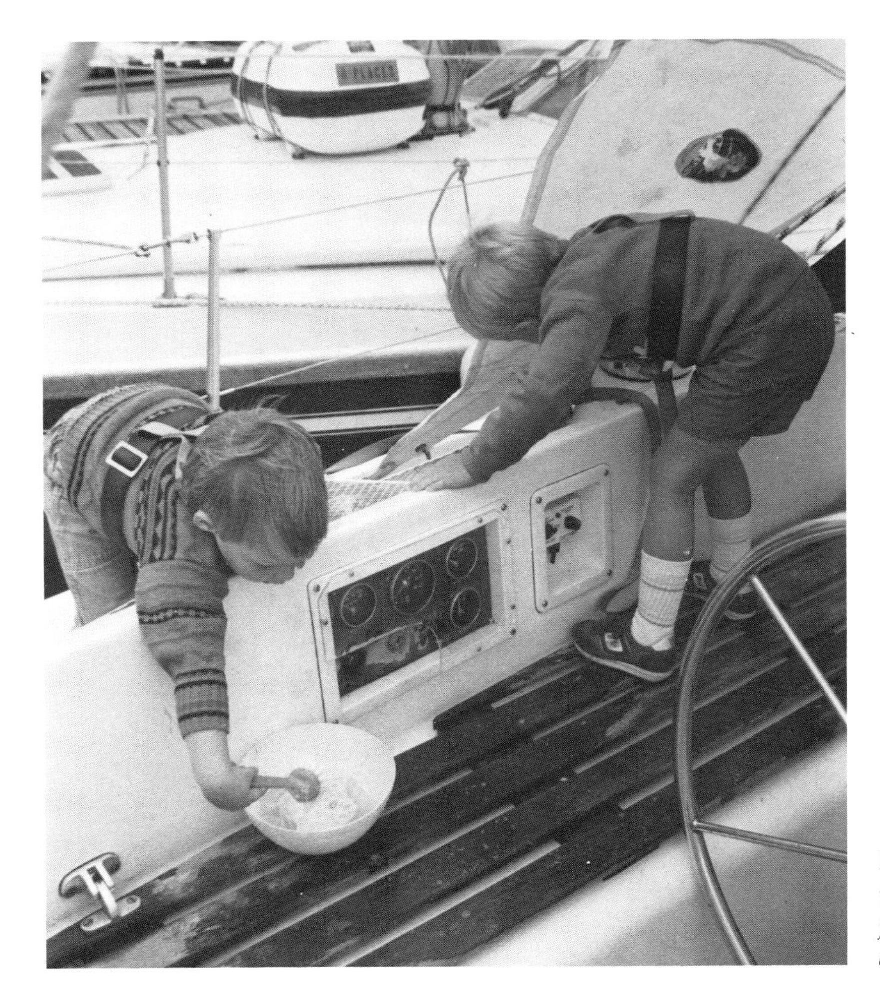

Left: Water, brushes and soap will keep the deck washers busy for ages – but remember to close all hatches first!

Learning to sail

Strange as it may seem, a cruising yacht is not the best place for a child to learn to sail. Background knowledge is picked up in the course of family cruising but, if you really want a child to learn the techniques for himself, it is better to start in a dinghy.

In common with parents elsewhere in Europe and in the United States, we have the ability to encourage our children to learn the basic skills of sailing from the age of six (or thereabouts) in the boat specially designed for youngsters, the International Optimist. With more than a quarter of a million boats in almost fifty countries, the Optimist has proved itself as a junior trainer. Many sailing clubs and schools have fleets of boats and provide training courses to introduce young sailors to the principles of the sport. Don't think you've got to teach your children yourself; in fact, it's probably better if you don't. Leave it to the club or school instructors who know exactly what they are doing and have well-established teaching routines.

The same advice about starting in a dinghy applies to older children and, for that matter, to adults too. It's not just that early mistakes will be less damaging in a simple, light dinghy than in a heavy yacht, but someone who learns the basic techniques in a responsive dinghy will be a more sensitive sailor.

When it comes to learning about cruising, there are three ways of doing it. It's likely that your children will learn directly from cruising with you, but there may be a time when you consider the other options (possibly for yourself, too). The first is to opt for a cruising school. Typically, these run five-day courses at various levels to cater for everyone from novices to those needing skippering experience or offshore racing knowledge.

Although I haven't heard of many cruising parents who have sent their children on courses like these, there are plenty of precedents for women taking such courses in order to learn more about boat handling and skippering. In fact anyone cruising regularly with a Captain Bligh partner who is reluctant to hand over the wheel and thinks of women as galley slaves is strongly recommended to take a break and learn from a professional instructor. In the UK, the best schools are recognised by the Royal Yachting Association, who train the instructors and inspect the yachts to ensure that standards of safety and tuition are maintained.

Apart from learning by experience or from a sailing school, the final option for youngsters is to take one of the many opportunities offered by the various sea training organisations. Make the initial contact through your national authority.

The motives of those who run these organisations may be rather different from those of the professional sailing school instructor, and indeed from each other. They all, however, share the belief that the sea provides a challenging environment in which young people may learn a whole range of things, not simply about sailing but about themselves, each other and about life. Come to think about it, isn't that exactly why we take children afloat?

Below: Cruising keeps the young family together. On passage, there's always time for a cuddle or a chat, away from the pressures of home, school and work.

Also published by Fernhurst Books

Sailing: A Beginner's Manual *John Driscoll*
Sailing the Mirror *Roy Partridge*
Topper Sailing *John Caig*
The Laser Book *Tim Davison*
Laser Racing *Ed Baird*
Boardsailing: A Beginner's Manual *John Heath*
Board Racing *Geoff Turner & Tim Davison*
Dee Caldwell's Book of Freestyle Boardsailing *Dee Caldwell*

Sail to Win

Tactics *Rodney Pattisson*
Dinghy Helming *Lawrie Smith*
Dinghy Crewing *Julian Brooke-Houghton*
Wind Strategy *David Houghton*
Tuning Your Dinghy *Lawrie Smith*
The Rules in Practice *Bryan Willis*
Tides and Currents *David Arnold*
Boatspeed – Supercharging your hull, foils and gear *Rodney Pattison*
Sails *John Heyes*
The Winning Mind – Strategies for successful sailing *John Whitmore*

Yachting

Weather at Sea *David Houghton*
Inshore Navigation *Tom Cunliffe*
Marine VHF Operation *Michael Gale*
Heavy Weather Cruising *Tom Cunliffe*
Yacht Skipper *Robin Aisher*
Yacht Crewing *Malcolm McKeag*
Tuning Yachts and Small Keelboats *Lawrie Smith*
Motor Boating *Alex McMullen*
Electronic Navigation *Mik Chinery*
Celestial Navigation *Tom Cunliffe*

If you would like to receive regular information about our new and forthcoming books, please send your name and address to:

Fernhurst Books, 31 Church Road, Hove,
East Sussex, BN3 2FA